Lives of the
Necromancers

Lives of the Necromancers

EDITED WITH
INTRODUCTIONS

William Godwin

Anthony Comegna, Editor

LIBERTARIANISM.ORG
WASHINGTON, DC

CONTENTS

Introduction   1

1. *Penetrating Futurity and Commanding Events*   15

2. *Necromancy, Alchemy, and Hallucinogenic Cults*   28

3. *The Fraudsters of Ancient Greece*   39

4. *Liars and Legends in Ancient Rome*   53

5. *Magic and Mysticism in the "East" from Zoroaster to "Arabian Nights"*   67

6. *Merlin, Dunstan, and Dark Age Britain*   80

7. *Papal Sorcerers and Technocrats in Medieval Europe*   97

8. *Albertus Magnus, Roger Bacon, and the Alchemy Cult*   111

9. *Joan of Arc & the Witch Hunters*   129

10. *The Life and Times of Dr. Faust*   150

11. *Quacks & Hucksters*   170

12. *King James & Matthew Hopkins: Witch Finders*   191

13. *Witch Trials in Sweden & Salem*   208

Introduction

Though he is somewhat little discussed today, William Godwin was and remains one of the most brilliant radical liberal writers of his age. He is considered by many the first modern anarchist, and his writings of all kinds earned him renown and great respect in his day. A true and shining example of Enlightenment-era skepticism, Godwin devoted much of his career to dispelling ignorance, myths, half-truths, and lies of all sorts. His 1834 *Lives of the Necromancers* ("or, An Account of the Most Eminent Persons in Successive Ages Who Have Claimed for Themselves or to Whom Has Been Imputed by Others the Exercise of Magical Powers") is an especially important foray into philosophy, cosmology, and psychology. Throughout the volume, Godwin investigates examples of supernatural beliefs throughout world history. His purpose was "to exhibit a fair delineation of the credulity of the human mind:" an intellectual inoculation for his popular audience against poisonously bad ideas. Across the Atlantic, Edgar Allan Poe reviewed *Lives of the Necromancers*, remarking that Godwin's writing exhibited "an air of mature thought—of deliberate premeditation pervading, in a remarkable degree, even his most common-place observations." In Godwin's hands, the most banal cultural myths, legends, and institutions became outright lies and well orchestrated aristocratic deceptions. Poe commented that "No English writer...with the single exception of Coleridge, has a fuller appreciation of the value of words." The American literatus continued: "His compilation is an invaluable work, evincing much labor and research, and full of absorbing interest." "The only drawback," Poe concluded with mournful respect, "is found in the author's unwelcome announcement in the Preface, that for the present he winds up his literary labors with the production of this book." Godwin's most insightful pen, he declared, "should never for a moment be idle." It is in that spirit that we republish Godwin's fascinating, challenging, and enlightening study of all things occult. To give readers both a pleasurable *and* insightful experience, this volume has been abridged and annotated. Readers who, like Poe, find themselves taken with Godwin are *strongly* encouraged to read the full volume, which is widely available for free on the Internet.

Preface

The main purpose of this book is to exhibit a fair

delineation of the credulity of the human mind. Such an exhibition cannot fail to be productive of the most salutary lessons....

Nothing can be more striking than the contrast between man and the inferior animals. The latter live only for the day, and see for the most part only what is immediately before them. But man lives in the past and the future. He reasons upon and improves by the past; he records the acts of a long series of generations: and he looks into future time, lays down plans which he shall be months and years in bringing to maturity, and contrives machines and delineates systems of education and government, which may gradually add to the accommodations of all, and raise the species generally into a nobler and more honourable character than our ancestors were capable of sustaining.

Man looks through nature, and is able to reduce its parts into a great whole. He classes the beings which are found in it, both animate and inanimate, delineates and describes them, investigates their properties, and records their capacities, their good and evil qualities, their dangers and their uses.

Nor does he only see all that is; but he also images all that is not. He takes to pieces the substances that are, and combines their parts into new arrangements. He peoples all the elements from the world of his imagination. It is here that he is most extraordinary and wonderful. The record of what actually is, and has happened in the series of human events, is perhaps the smallest part of human history. If we would know man in all his subtleties, we must deviate into the world of miracles and sorcery. To know the things that are not, and cannot be, but have been imagined and believed, is the most curious chapter in the annals of man. To observe the actual results of these imaginary phenomena, and the crimes and cruelties they have caused us to commit, is one of the most instructive studies in which we can possibly be engaged. It is here that man is most astonishing, and that we contemplate with most admiration the discursive and unbounded nature of his faculties.

But, if a recollection of the examples of the credulity of the human mind may in one view supply nourishment to our pride, it still more obviously tends to teach us sobriety and humiliation. Man in his genuine and direct sphere is the disciple of reason; it is by this faculty that he draws inferences, exerts his prudence, and displays the ingenuity of machinery, and the subtlety of system both in natural and moral philosophy. Yet what so irrational as man? Not contented with making use of the powers we possess, for the purpose of conducing to our accommodation and well being, we with a daring spirit inquire into the invisible causes of what we see, and people all nature with Gods "of every shape and size" and angels, with principalities and powers, with beneficent beings who "take charge concerning us lest at any time we dash our foot against a stone," and with devils who are perpetually on the watch to perplex us and do us injury. And, having familiarised our minds with the conceptions of these beings, we immediately aspire to hold communion with them. We represent to ourselves God, as "walking in the garden with us in the cool of the day," and teach ourselves "not to forget to entertain strangers, lest by so doing we should repel angels unawares."

No sooner are we, even in a slight degree, acquainted with the laws of nature, than we frame to ourselves the idea, by the aid of some invisible ally, of suspending their operation, of calling out meteors in the sky, of commanding storms and tempests, of arresting the motion of the heavenly bodies, of producing miraculous cures upon the bodies of our fellow-men, or afflicting them with disease and death, of calling up the deceased from the silence of the grave, and compelling them to disclose "the secrets of the world unknown."

But, what is most deplorable, we are not contented to endeavour to secure the aid of God and good angels, but we also aspire to enter into alliance with devils, and beings destined for their rebellion to suffer eternally the pains of hell. As they are supposed to be of a character perverted and depraved, we of course apply to them principally for purposes of wantonness, or of malice and revenge. And, in the instances which have occurred only a few centuries back, the most common idea has been of a compact entered into by an unprincipled and impious human being with the sworn enemy of God and man, in the result of which the devil engages to serve the capricious will and perform the behests of his blasphemous votary for a certain number of years, while the deluded wretch in return engages to renounce his God and Saviour, and surrender himself body and soul to the pains of hell from the end of that term to all eternity. No sooner do we imagine human beings invested with these wonderful powers, and conceive them as called into action for the most malignant purposes, than we become the passive and terrified slaves of the creatures of our own imaginations, and fear to be assailed at every moment by beings to whose power we can set no limit, and whose modes of hostility no human sagacity can anticipate and provide against. But, what is still more extraordinary, the human creatures that pretend to these powers have often been found as completely the dupes of this supernatural machinery, as the most timid wretch that stands in terror at its expected operation; and no phenomenon has been more common than the confession of these allies of hell, that they have verily and indeed held commerce and formed plots and conspiracies with Satan.

The consequence of this state of things has been, that criminal jurisprudence and the last severities of the law have been called forth to an amazing extent to exterminate witches and witchcraft. More especially in the sixteenth century hundreds and thousands were burned alive within the compass of a small territory; and judges, the directors of the scene, a Nicholas Remi, a De Lancre, and many others, have published copious volumes, entering into a minute detail of the system and fashion of the witchcraft of the professors, whom they sent in multitudes to expiate their depravity at the gallows and the stake.

One useful lesson which we may derive from the detail of these particulars, is the folly in most cases of imputing pure and unmingled hypocrisy to man. The human mind is of so ductile a character that, like what is affirmed of charity by the apostle, it "believeth all things, and endureth all things." We are not at liberty to trifle with the sacredness of truth. While we persuade others, we begin to deceive ourselves. Human life is a drama of that sort, that, while we act our part, and endeavour to do justice to the sentiments which are put down for us, we begin to believe we are the thing we would represent.

To shew however the modes in which the delusion acts upon the person through whom it operates, is not properly the scope of this book. Here and there I have suggested hints to this purpose, which the curious reader may follow to their furthest extent, and discover how with perfect good faith the artist may bring himself to swallow the grossest impossibilities. But the work I have written is not a treatise of natural magic. It rather proposes to display the immense wealth of the faculty of imagination, and to shew the extravagances of which the man may be guilty who surrenders himself to its guidance.

It is fit however that the reader should bear in mind, that what is put down in this book is but a small part and scantling of the acts of sorcery and witchcraft which have existed in human society. They have been found in all ages and countries. The torrid zone and the frozen north have neither of them escaped from a fruitful harvest of this sort of offspring. In ages of ignorance they have been especially at home; and the races of men that have left no records behind them to tell almost that they existed, have been most of all rife in deeds of darkness, and those marvellous incidents which especially astonish the spectator, and throw back the infant reason of man into those shades and that obscurity from which it had so recently endeavoured to escape.

I wind up for the present my literary labours with the production of this book. Nor let any reader imagine that I here put into his hands a mere work of idle recreation. It will be found pregnant with deeper uses. The wildest extravagances of human fancy, the most deplorable perversion of human faculties, and the most horrible distortions of jurisprudence, may occasionally afford us a salutary lesson. I love in the foremost place to contemplate man in all his honours and in all the exaltation of wisdom and virtue; but it will also be occasionally of service to us to look into his obliquities, and distinctly to remark how great and portentous have been his absurdities and his follies.

May 29, 1834.

Introduction

The improvements that have been effected in natural

philosophy have by degrees convinced the enlightened part of mankind that the material universe is every where subject to laws, fixed in their weight, measure and duration, capable of the most exact calculation, and which in no case admit of variation and exception. Whatever is not thus to be accounted for is of mind, and springs from the volition of some being, of which the material form is subjected to our senses, and the action of which is in like manner regulated by the laws of matter. Beside this, mind, as well as matter, is subject to fixed laws; and thus every phenomenon and occurrence around us is rendered a topic for the speculations of sagacity and foresight. Such is the creed which science has universally prescribed to the judicious and reflecting among us.

It was otherwise in the infancy and less mature state of human knowledge. The chain of causes and consequences was yet unrecognized; and events perpetually occurred, for which no sagacity that was then in being was able to assign an original. Hence men felt themselves habitually disposed to refer many of the appearances with which they were conversant to the agency of invisible intelligences; sometimes under the influence of a benignant disposition, sometimes of malice, and sometimes perhaps from an inclination to make themselves sport of the wonder and astonishment of ignorant mortals. Omens and portents told these men of some piece of good or ill fortune speedily to befal them. The flight of birds was watched by them, as foretokening somewhat important. Thunder excited in them a feeling of supernatural terror. Eclipses with fear of change perplexed the nations. The phenomena of the heavens, regular and irregular, were anxiously remarked from the same principle. During the hours of darkness men were apt to see a supernatural being in every bush; and they could not cross a receptacle for the dead, without expecting to encounter some one of the departed uneasily wandering among graves, or commissioned to reveal somewhat momentous and deeply affecting to the survivors. Fairies danced in the moonlight glade; and something preternatural perpetually occurred to fill the living with admiration and awe.

All this gradually reduced itself into a system. Mankind, particularly in the dark and ignorant ages, were divided into the strong and the weak; the strong and weak of animal frame, when corporeal strength more decidedly bore sway than in a period of greater cultivation; and the strong and weak in reference to intellect; those who were bold, audacious and enterprising in acquiring an ascendancy over their fellowmen, and those who truckled, submitted, and were acted upon, from an innate consciousness of inferiority, and a superstitious looking up to such as were of greater natural or acquired endowments than themselves. The strong in intellect were eager to avail themselves of their superiority, by means that escaped the penetration of the multitude, and had recourse to various artifices to effect their ends. Beside this, they became the dupes of their own practices. They set out at first in their conception of things from the level of the vulgar. They applied themselves diligently to the unravelling of what was unknown; wonder mingled with their contemplation; they abstracted their minds from things of ordinary occurrence, and, as we may denominate it, of real life, till at length they lost their true balance amidst the astonishment they sought to produce in their inferiors. They felt a vocation to things extraordinary; and they willingly gave scope and line without limit to that which engendered in themselves the most gratifying sensations, at the same time that it answered the purposes of their ambition.

As these principles in the two parties, the more refined and the vulgar, are universal, and derive their origin from the nature of man, it has necessarily happened that this faith in extraordinary events, and superstitious fear of what is supernatural, has diffused itself through every climate of the world, in a certain stage of human intellect, and while refinement had not yet got the better of barbarism....

The history of mankind therefore will be very imperfect, and our knowledge of the operations and eccentricities of the mind lamentably deficient, unless we take into our view what has occurred under this head. The supernatural appearances with which our ancestors conceived themselves perpetually surrounded must have had a strong tendency to cherish and keep alive the powers of the imagination, and to penetrate those who witnessed or expected such things with an extraordinary sensitiveness. As the course of events appears to us at present, there is much, though abstractedly within the compass of human sagacity to foresee, which yet the actors on the scene do not foresee: but the blindness and perplexity of short-sighted mortals must have been wonderfully increased, when ghosts and extraordinary appearances were conceived liable to cross the steps and confound the projects of men at every turn, and a malicious wizard or a powerful enchanter might involve his unfortunate victim in a chain of calamities, which no prudence could disarm, and no virtue could deliver him from. They were the slaves of an uncontrolable destiny, and must therefore have been eminently deficient in the perseverance and moral courage, which may justly be required of us in a more enlightened age. And the men (but these were few compared with the great majority of mankind), who believed themselves gifted with supernatural endowments, must have felt exempt and privileged from common rules, somewhat in the same way as the persons whom fiction has delighted to pourtray as endowed with immeasurable wealth, or with the power of rendering themselves impassive or invisible. But, whatever were their advantages or disadvantages, at any rate it is good for us to call up in review things, which are now passed away, but which once occupied so large a share of the thoughts and attention of mankind, and in a great degree tended to modify their characters and dictate their resolutions....

Nor only is this subject inexpressibly interesting, as

setting before us how the loftiest and most enterprising minds of ancient days formerly busied themselves.
It is also of the highest importance to an ingenuous
curiosity, inasmuch as it vitally affected the fortunes of
so considerable a portion of the mass of mankind. The
legislatures of remote ages bent all their severity at different periods against what they deemed the unhallowed arts of the sons and daughters of reprobation.
Multitudes of human creatures have been sacrificed in
different ages and countries, upon the accusation of
having exercised arts of the most immoral and sacrilegious character. They were supposed to have formed
a contract with a mighty and invisible spirit, the great
enemy of man, and to have sold themselves, body and
soul, to everlasting perdition, for the sake of gratifying, for a short term of years, their malignant passions against those who had been so unfortunate as
to give them cause of offence. If there were any persons who imagined they had entered into such a contract, however erroneous was their belief, they must of
necessity have been greatly depraved. And it was but
natural that such as believed in this crime, must have
considered it as atrocious beyond all others, and have
regarded those who were supposed guilty of it with
inexpressible abhorrence. There are many instances
on record, where the persons accused of it, either from
the depth of their delusion, or, which is more probable, harassed by persecution, by the hatred of their
fellow-creatures directed against them, or by torture,
actually confessed themselves guilty. These instances

are too numerous, not to constitute an important chapter in the legislation of past ages. And, now that the illusion has in a manner passed away from the face of the earth, we are on that account the better qualified to investigate this error in its causes and consequences, and to look back on the tempest and hurricane from which we have escaped, with chastened feelings, and a sounder estimate of its nature, its reign, and its effects.

1

Penetrating Futurity and Commanding Events

From the first entries, our learned, enlightened author begins his empiricist, rationalist attack on all things supernatural. Godwin believed that Nature, properly conceived, encompasses all things and through man's unique powers of reason we can divine Nature's laws. Throughout the ages and into the very mists of human existence, however, there have been those who seek to obfuscate and obscure from individuals the power to reason. The charismatic, the cunning, and the immoral seekers after power have, from time immemorial, organized themselves into classes of conspirators against the liberties and wisdom of the common people. Godwin's *Lives of the Necromancers* was an attempt to disarm these classes of priests, magicians, fortune tellers, divine-right monarchs, and lickspittle court devotionists; to dispel the mysticisms which clouded common people's minds, from astrology and physiognomy to the psychology of dreams and cold-reading hucksters. Behind it all, sadly and unfortunately, lay the "boundless ambition" of even the most average of people. Because practically everyone can be swept away with grandiose dreams and visions of the supernatural and the real blending together, practically everyone falls prey to those who would lie, cheat, and worse to dominate their fellow beings. It is then the role of the educator to dispel the myths which accumulate like so many cobwebs in the corners of the mind, steadily shrinking the bounds of mental life. Godwin begins his encyclopedic Spring cleaning by detailing humanity's desire to attain ever-greater power and knowledge, so much so that they may even predict and control the future.

Ambitious Nature of Man

Man is a creature of boundless ambition.

It is probably our natural wants that first awaken us from that lethargy and indifference in which man may be supposed to be plunged previously to the impulse of any motive, or the accession of any uneasiness. One of our earliest wants may be conceived to be hunger, or the desire of food.

From this simple beginning the history of man in all its complex varieties may be regarded as proceeding.

Man in a state of society, more especially where there is an inequality of condition and rank, is very often the creature of leisure. He finds in himself, either from internal or external impulse, a certain activity. He finds himself at one time engaged in the accomplishment of his obvious and immediate desires, and at another in a state in which these desires have for the present been fulfilled, and he has no present occasion to repeat those exertions which led to their fulfilment. This is the period of contemplation. This is the state which most eminently distinguishes us from the brutes. Here it is that the history of man, in its exclusive sense, may be considered as taking its beginning.

Here it is that he specially recognises in himself the sense of power. Power in its simplest acceptation, may be exerted in either of two ways, either in his procuring for himself an ample field for more refined accommodations, or in the exercise of compulsion and authority over other living creatures. In the pursuit of either of these, and especially the first, he is led to the attainment of skill and superior adroitness in the use of his faculties.

No sooner has man reached to this degree of

17

improvement, than now, if not indeed earlier, he is induced to remark the extreme limitedness of his faculties in respect to the future; and he is led, first earnestly to desire a clearer insight into the future, and next a power of commanding those external causes upon which the events of the future depend. The first of these desires is the parent of divination, augury, chiromancy, astrology, and the consultation of oracles; and the second has been the prolific source of enchantment, witchcraft, sorcery, magic, necromancy, and alchemy, in its two branches, the unlimited prolongation of human life, and the art of converting less precious metals into gold.

His Desire to Penetrate into Futurity.

Nothing can suggest to us a more striking and stupendous idea of the faculties of the human mind, than the consideration of the various arts by which men have endeavoured to penetrate into the future, and to command the events of the future, in ways that in sobriety and truth are entirely out of our competence. We spurn impatiently against the narrow limits which the constitution of things has fixed to our aspirings, and endeavour by a multiplicity of ways to accomplish that which it is totally beyond the power of man to effect…

Physiognomy.

Physiognomy is not so properly a prediction of future events, as an attempt to explain the present and inherent qualities of a man. By unfolding his propensities however, it virtually gave the world to understand the sort of proceedings in which he was most likely to engage. The story of Socrates and the physiognomist is sufficiently known. The physiognomist having inspected the countenance of the philosopher, pronounced that he was given to intemperance, sensuality, and violent bursts of passion, all of which was so contrary to his character as universally known, that his disciples derided the physiognomist as a vain-glorious pretender. Socrates however presently put them to silence, by declaring that he had had an original propensity to all the vices imputed to him, and had only conquered the propensity by dint of a severe and unremitted self-discipline.

Interpretation of Dreams.

Oneirocriticism, or the art of interpreting dreams, seems of all the modes of prediction the most inseparable from the nature of man. A considerable portion of every twenty-four hours of our lives is spent in sleep; and in sleep nothing is at least more usual, than for the mind to be occupied in a thousand imaginary scenes, which for the time are as realities, and often excite the passions of the mind of the sleeper in no ordinary degree. Many of them are wild and rambling; but many also have a portentous sobriety. Many seem to have a strict connection with the incidents of our actual lives; and some appear as if they came for the very purpose to warn us of danger, or prepare us for coming events. It is therefore no wonder that these occasionally fill our waking thoughts with a deep interest, and impress upon us an anxiety of which we feel it difficult to rid ourselves. Accordingly, in ages when men were more prone to superstition, than at present, they sometimes constituted a subject of earnest anxiety and inquisitiveness; and we find among the earliest exercises of the art of prediction, the interpretation of dreams to have occupied a principal place, and to have been as it were reduced into a science...

Astrology.

Astrology was one of the modes most anciently and universally resorted to for discovering the fortunes of men and nations. Astronomy and astrology went hand in hand, particularly among the people of the East. The idea of fate was most especially bound up in this branch of prophecy. If the fortune of a man was intimately connected with the position of the heavenly bodies, it became evident that little was left to the province of his free will. The stars overruled him in all his determinations; and it was in vain for him to resist them. There was something flattering to the human imagination in conceiving that the planets and the orbs on high were concerned in the conduct we should pursue, and the events that should befal us. Man resigned himself to his fate with a solemn, yet a lofty feeling, that the remotest portions of the universe were concerned in the catastrophe that awaited him. Beside which, there was something peculiarly seducing in the apparently profound investigation of the professors of astrology. They busied themselves with the actual position of the heavenly bodies, their conjunctions and oppositions; and of consequence there was a great apparatus of diagrams and calculation to which they were prompted to apply themselves, and which addressed itself to the eyes and imaginations of those who consulted them.

Oracles.

But that which seems to have had the greatest vogue in times of antiquity, relative to the prediction of future events, is what is recorded of oracles. Finding the insatiable curiosity of mankind as to what was to happen hereafter, and the general desire they felt to be guided in their conduct by an anticipation of things to come, the priests pretty generally took advantage of this passion, to increase their emoluments and offerings, and the more effectually to inspire the rest of their species with veneration and a willing submission to their authority. The oracle was delivered in a temple, or some sacred place; and in this particular we plainly discover that mixture of nature and art, of genuine enthusiasm and contriving craft, which is so frequently exemplified in the character of man.

Delphi.

The oracle of Apollo at Delphi is the most remarkable....A goat-herd fed his flocks on the acclivity of mount Parnassus. As the animals wandered here and there in pursuit of food, they happened to approach a deep and long chasm which appeared in the rock. From this chasm a vapour issued; and the goats had no sooner inhaled a portion of the vapour, than they began to play and frisk about with singular agility. The goat-herd, observing this, and curious to discover the cause, held his head over the chasm; when, in a short time, the fumes having ascended to his brain, he threw himself into a variety of strange attitudes, and uttered words, which probably he did not understand himself, but which were supposed to convey a prophetic meaning.

This phenomenon was taken advantage of, and a temple to Apollo was erected on the spot. The credulous many believed that here was obviously a centre and focus of divine inspiration....The apartment of the oracle was immediately over the chasm from which the vapour issued. A priestess delivered the responses...She sat upon a tripod, or three-legged stool, perforated with holes, over the seat of the vapours. After a time, her figure enlarged itself, her hair stood on end, her complexion and features became altered, her heart panted and her bosom swelled, and her voice grew more than human. In this condition she uttered a number of wild and incoherent phrases, which were supposed to be dictated by the God. The questions which were offered by those who came to consult the oracle were then proposed to her, and her answers taken down by the priest, whose office was to arrange and methodize them, and put them into hexameter verse, after which they were delivered to the votaries. The priestess could only be consulted on one day in every month.

Great ingenuity and contrivance were no doubt required to uphold the credit of the oracle; and no less boldness and self-collectedness on the part of those by whom the machinery was conducted. Like the conjurors of modern times, they took care to be extensively informed as to all such matters respecting which the oracle was likely to be consulted. They listened probably to the Pythia with a superstitious reverence for the incoherent sentences she uttered. She, like them, spent her life in being trained for the office to which she was devoted. All that was rambling and inapplicable in her wild declamation they consigned to oblivion. Whatever seemed to bear on the question proposed they preserved. The persons by whom the responses were digested into hexameter verse, had of course a commission attended with great discretionary power...The oracles accordingly reached to so high a degree of reputation, that, as Cicero observes, no expedition for a long time was undertaken, no colony sent out, and often no affair of any distinguished family or individual entered on, without the previously obtaining their judgment and sanction...

The Desire to Command and Control Future Events.

Next to the consideration of those measures by which men have sought to dive into the secrets of future time, the question presents itself of those more daring undertakings, the object of which has been by some supernatural power to control the future, and place it in subjection to the will of the unlicensed adventurer. Men have always, especially in ages of ignorance, and when they most felt their individual weakness, figured to themselves an invisible strength greater than their own; and, in proportion to their impatience, and the fervour of their desires, have sought to enter into a league with those beings whose mightier force might supply that in which their weakness failed.

Commerce with the Invisible World.

...In Egypt and throughout the East, especially in the early periods of history, the supposed commerce with invisible powers was openly professed, which, under other circumstances, and during the reign of different prejudices, was afterwards carefully concealed, and barbarously hunted out of the pale of allowed and authorised practice. The Magi of old, who claimed a power of producing miraculous appearances, and boasted a familiar intercourse with the world of spirits, were regarded by their countrymen with peculiar reverence, and considered as the first and chiefest men in the state. For this mitigated view of such dark and mysterious proceedings the ancients were in a great degree indebted to their polytheism. The Romans are computed to have acknowledged thirty thousand divinities, to all of whom was rendered a legitimate homage; and other countries in a similar proportion...

Witchcraft.

...The sorcerer... was frequently a man of learning and intellectual abilities, sometimes of comparative opulence and respectable situation in society. But the witch or wizard was almost uniformly old, decrepid, and nearly or altogether in a state of penury...They appear in most cases to have been brought into action by the impulse of private malice. They occasioned mortality of greater or less extent in man and beast. They blighted the opening prospect of a plentiful harvest. They covered the heavens with clouds, and sent abroad withering and malignant blasts. They undermined the health of those who were so unfortunate as to incur their animosity, and caused them to waste away gradually with incurable disease. They were notorious two or three centuries ago for the power of the "evil eye." The vulgar, both great and small, dreaded their displeasure, and sought, by small gifts, and fair speeches, but insincere, and the offspring of terror only, to avert the pernicious consequences of their malice…

Compacts with the Devil.

The power of these witches, as we find in their earliest records, originated in their intercourse with "familiar spirits," invisible beings who must be supposed to be enlisted in the armies of the prince of darkness. We do not read in these ancient memorials of any league of mutual benefit entered into between the merely human party, and his or her supernatural assistant. But modern times have amply supplied this defect. The witch or sorcerer could not secure the assistance of the demon but by a sure and faithful compact, by which the human party obtained the industrious and vigilant service of his familiar for a certain term of years, only on condition that, when the term was expired, the demon of undoubted right was to obtain possession of the indentured party, and to convey him irremissibly and for ever to the regions of the damned. The contract was drawn out in authentic form, signed by the sorcerer, and attested with his blood, and was then carried away by the demon, to be produced again at the appointed time.

Imps.

...subordinate devils were called Imps. Impure and carnal ideas were mingled with these theories. The witches were said to have preternatural teats from which their familiars sucked their blood. The devil also engaged in sexual intercourse with the witch or wizard, being denominated incubus, if his favourite were a woman, and succubus, if a man. In short, every frightful and loathsome idea was carefully heaped up together, to render the unfortunate beings to whom the crime of witchcraft was imputed the horror and execration of their species.

Talismans and Amulets.

As according to the doctrine of witchcraft, there were certain compounds, and matters prepared by rules of art, that proved baleful and deadly to the persons against whom their activity was directed, so there were also preservatives, talismans, amulets and charms, for the most [part] to be worn about the person, which rendered him superior to injury, not only from the operations of witchcraft, but in some cases from the sword or any other mortal weapon...in the midst of every tremendous assailant, "might pass on with unblenched majesty," uninjured and invulnerable.

2

Necromancy, Alchemy, and Hallucinogenic Cults

Many entries into the text, we finally broach the titular subject: contact with the dead and attempts throughout the Near East to manipulate the natural world. The necromancer's dark disturbance of the deceased violated the broadly accepted laws of ethics and religious sentiment. Only those individuals motivated by the most wicked and horrifying lusts would resort to such unnatural means of acquiring power. No less batty—though decidedly more benign—were the alchemists, Rosicrucians, Magi, and a variety of other Egyptian and Middle Eastern priesthoods. The alchemist promised both unending wealth *and* immortality, and in search of these grandiose dreams the Rosicrucians appear to have indulged in hallucinogenic communications with elemental creatures. Godwin writes that the priests would attempt to purge "the organs of human sight" with a "universal medicine, and that certain glass globes should be chemically prepared with one or other of the four elements." Upon completion of the ritual, "the initiated immediately had a sight of innumerable beings of a luminous substance, but of thin and evanescent structure, that people the elements on all sides of us." As leading initiates claimed the ability to control these fearsome beings, they commanded the full loyalty of their subordinate priests. From further east and of far more ancient origins, the Magi reportedly engaged in similarly cultish communications with the gods to enforce the priestly hierarchy. Godwin explains this phenomenon by noting that before the dawn of modernity, scientific knowledge was reserved exclusively for elites and a very small number of specialists. In this atmosphere of monopolized knowledge about science and technology, the cunning clerisy sharply separated and insulated themselves from the vast herd of common laborers and even those of middling status within the ruling class itself. The divisions between the ruling and exploitative few and the ruled, exploited many were so stark that conquerors like Alexander lived on after death, venerated as a god incarnate.

Ambitious Nature of Man

Necromancy.

...There is something sacred to common apprehension in the repose of the dead. They seem placed beyond our power to disturb. "There is no work, nor device, nor knowledge, nor wisdom in the grave..."

Their remains moulder in the earth. Neither form nor feature is long continued to them. We shrink from their touch, and their sight. To violate the sepulchre therefore for the purpose of unholy spells and operations, as we read of in the annals of witchcraft, cannot fail to be exceedingly shocking. To call up the spirits of the departed, after they have fulfilled the task of life, and are consigned to their final sleep, is sacrilegious. Well may they exclaim, like the ghost of Samuel in the sacred story, "Why hast thou disquieted me?"

There is a further circumstance in the case, which causes us additionally to revolt from the very idea of necromancy, strictly so called. Man is a mortal, or an immortal being. His frame either wholly "returns to the earth as it was, or his spirit," the thinking principle within him, "to God who gave it." The latter is the prevailing sentiment of mankind in modern times. Man is placed upon earth in a state of probation, to be dealt with hereafter according to the deeds done in the flesh. "Some shall go away into everlasting punishment; and others into life eternal." In this case there is something blasphemous in the idea of intermedding with the state of the dead. We must leave them in the hands of God. Even on the idea of an interval, the "sleep of the soul" from death to the general resurrection, which is the creed of no contemptible sect of Christians, it is surely a terrific notion that we should disturb the pause, which upon that hypothesis, the laws of nature have assigned to the departed soul, and come to awake, or to "torment him before the time."

Alchemy.

To make our catalogue of supernatural doings, and the lawless imaginations of man, the more complete, it may be further necessary to refer to the craft, so eagerly cultivated in successive ages of the world of converting the inferior metals into gold, to which was usually joined the elixir vitae, or universal medicine, having the quality of renewing the youth of man, and causing him to live for ever...

It is well known however how eagerly it was cultivated in various countries of the world for many centuries after it was divulged by Geber. Men of the most wonderful talents devoted their lives to the investigation; and in multiplied instances the discovery was said to have been completed. Vast sums of money were consumed in the fruitless endeavour; and in a later period it seems to have furnished an excellent handle to vain and specious projectors, to extort money from those more amply provided with the goods of fortune than themselves.

The art no doubt is in itself sufficiently mystical, having been pursued by multitudes, who seemed to themselves ever on the eve of consummation, but as constantly baffled when to their own apprehension most on the verge of success. The discovery indeed appears upon the face of it to be of the most delicate nature, as the benefit must wholly depend upon its being reserved to one or a very few, the object being unbounded wealth, which is nothing unless confined. If the power of creating gold is diffused, wealth by such diffusion becomes poverty, and every thing after a short time would but return to what it had been. Add to which, that the nature of discovery has ordinarily been, that, when once the clue has been found, it reveals itself to several about the same period of time...

Rosicrucians.

Nothing very distinct has been ascertained respecting a sect, calling itself Rosicrucians. It is said to have originated in the East from one of the crusaders in the fourteenth century; but it attracted at least no public notice till the beginning of the seventeenth century. Its adherents appear to have imbibed their notions from the Arabians, and claimed the possession of the philosopher's stone, the art of transmuting metals, and the elixir vitae.

Sylphs and Gnomes, Salamanders and Undines.

But that for which they principally excited public
attention, was their creed respecting certain elemen-
tary beings, which to grosser eyes are invisible, but
were familiarly known to the initiated. To be admitted to their acquaintance it was previously necessary
that the organs of human sight should be purged by
the universal medicine, and that certain glass globes
should be chemically prepared with one or other of
the four elements, and for one month exposed to the
beams of the sun. These preliminary steps being taken,
the initiated immediately had a sight of innumerable
beings of a luminous substance, but of thin and
evanescent structure, that people the elements on all
sides of us. Those who inhabited the air were called
Sylphs; and those who dwelt in the earth bore the
name of Gnomes; such as peopled the fire were Sala-
manders; and those who made their home in the
waters were Undines. Each class appears to have had
an extensive power in the elements to which they
belonged. They could raise tempests in the air, and
storms at sea, shake the earth, and alarm the inhabitants of the globe with the sight of devouring flames.
These appear however to have been more formidable
in appearance than in reality. And the whole race
was subordinate to man, and particularly subject to
the initiated. The gnomes, inhabitants of the earth
and the mines, liberally supplied to the human beings
with whom they conversed, the hidden treasures over

which they presided. The four classes were some of them male, and some female; but the female sex seems to have preponderated in all...

We should have taken but an imperfect survey of the lawless extravagancies of human imagination, if we had not included a survey of this sect. There is something particularly soothing to the fancy of an erratic mind, in the conception of being conversant with a race of beings the very existence of which is unperceived by ordinary mortals, and thus entering into an infinitely numerous and variegated society, even when we are apparently swallowed up in entire solitude...

Examples of Necromancy and Witchcraft from the Bible

The Magi, or Wise Men of the East.

The Magi, or Wise Men of the East, extended their ramifications over Egypt, Babylonia, Persia, India, and probably, though with a different name, over China, and indeed the whole known world. Their profession was of a mysterious nature. They laid claim to a familiar intercourse with the Gods. They placed themselves as mediators between heaven and earth, assumed the prerogative of revealing the will of beings of a nature superior to man, and pretended to show wonders and prodigies that surpassed any power which was merely human.

To understand this, we must bear in mind the state
of knowledge in ancient times, where for the most
part the cultivation of the mind, and an acquaintance
with either science or art, were confined to a very
small part of the population. In each of the nations we
have mentioned, there was a particular caste or tribe
of men, who, by the prerogative of their birth, were
entitled to the advantages of science and a superior
education, while the rest of their countrymen were
destined to subsist by manual labour. This of necessity gave birth in the privileged few to an overween-
ing sense of their own importance. They scarcely
regarded the rest of their countrymen as beings of the
same species with themselves; and, finding a strong
line of distinction cutting them off from the herd, they
had recourse to every practicable method for making that distinction still stronger. Wonder is one of
the most obvious means of generating deference; and,
by keeping to themselves the grounds and process
of their skill, and presenting the results only, they
were sure to excite the admiration and reverence of
their contemporaries. This mode of proceeding further produced a reaction upon themselves. That
which supplied and promised to supply to them so
large a harvest of honour and fame, unavoidably
became precious in their eyes. They pursued their
discoveries with avidity, because few had access to
their opportunities in that respect, and because, the
profounder were their researches, the more sure they
were of being looked up to by the public as having

that in them which was sacred and inviolable. They spent their days and nights in these investigations. They shrank from no privation and labour. At the same time that in these labours they had at all times an eye to their darling object, an ascendancy over the minds of their countrymen at large, and the extorting from them a blind and implicit deference to their oracular decrees. They however loved their pursuits for the pursuits themselves. They felt their abstraction and their unlimited nature, and on that account contemplated them with admiration. They valued them (for such is the indestructible character of the human mind) for the pains they had bestowed on them. The sweat of their brow grew into a part as it were of the intrinsic merit of the articles; and that which had with so much pains been attained by them, they could not but regard as of inestimable worth...

Temple of Jupiter Ammon: Its Oracles.

...This temple was situated at a distance of no less than twelve days' journey from Memphis, the capital of the Lower Egypt. The principal part of this space consisted of one immense tract of moving sand, so hot as to be intolerable to the sole of the foot, while the air was pregnant with fire, so that it was almost impossible to breathe in it. Not a drop of water, not a tree, not a blade of grass, was to be found through this vast surface. It was here that Cambyses, engaged in an impious expedition to demolish the temple, is

said to have lost an army of fifty thousand men, buried
in the sands. When you arrived however, you were
presented with a wood of great circumference, the
foliage of which was so thick that the beams of the
sun could not pierce it. The atmosphere of the place
was of a delicious temperature; the scene was every
where interspersed with fountains; and all the fruits
of the earth were found in the highest perfection. In
the midst was the temple and oracle of the God, who
was worshipped in the likeness of a ram. The Egyptian priests chose this site as furnishing a test of the zeal
of their votaries; the journey being like the pilgrimage
to Jerusalem or Mecca, if not from so great a distance,
yet attended in many respects with perils more formidable. It was not safe to attempt the passage but with
moderate numbers, and those expressly equipped for
expedition.

Bacchus is said to have visited this spot in his great
expedition to the East, when Jupiter appeared to him
in the form of a ram, having struck his foot upon
the soil, and for the first time occasioned that supply
of water, with which the place was ever after plentifully supplied. Alexander the Great in a subsequent
age undertook the same journey with his army, that
he might cause himself to be acknowledged for the
son of the God, under which character he was in all
due form recognised. The priests no doubt had heard
of the successful battles of the Granicus and of Issus, of
the capture of Tyre after a seven months' siege, and of

the march of the great conqueror in Egypt, where he carried every thing before him.

Here we are presented with a striking specimen of the mode and spirit in which the oracles of old were accustomed to be conducted. It may be said that the priests were corrupted by the rich presents which Alexander bestowed on them with a liberal hand. But this was not the prime impulse in the business. They were astonished at the daring with which Alexander with a comparative handful of men set out from Greece, having meditated the overthrow of the great Persian empire. They were astonished with his perpetual success, and his victorious progress from the Hellespont to mount Taurus, from mount Taurus to Pelusium, and from Pelusium quite across the ancient kingdom of Egypt to the Palus Mareotis. Accustomed to the practice of adulation, and to the belief that mortal power and true intellectual greatness were the same, they with a genuine enthusiastic fervour regarded Alexander as the son of their God, and acknowledged him as such.—Nothing can be more memorable than the way in which belief and unbelief hold a divided empire over the human mind, our passions hurrying us into belief, at the same time that our intervals of sobriety suggest to us that it is all pure imposition...

3

The Fraudsters of
Ancient Greece

Moving on from general concepts to the history of occult practice, our author explores the mystical life of the ancient Greeks. Godwin begins the section by restating his basic argument: "to the eye of uninstructed ignorance every thing is astonishing, every thing is unexpected." While legend might hold that Amphion could arrange stones on command with his lyre, the truth is probably far more mundane. Like the geometer and philosopher Pythagoras, Amphion was in all likelihood merely one of the few existing truly skilled engineers or architects in the Greek world. Pythagoras, in fact, was so brilliant that Godwin laments his rather bizarre pretensions to divinity. The great thinker commanded the worship of his followers, who gladly (for Godwin: *ignorantly*) followed his will. Between Pythagoras and his students, the master's word was unquestioned law. Thus did the master ensure that no students may ever take his place or surpass his grandeur. His student Epimenides, however, seems to have learned much. A man of apparently few scruples, Epimenides claimed to be in contact with invisible entities ("nymphs") and spirits that accorded him unique powers and abilities in our world. He was supposed to have practiced a sort of remote viewing or astral projection and seems to have supported himself by performing exorcisms throughout the countryside, restoring ruined farms to prosperity. But perhaps the most powerful of all ancient Greek cultists were the Oracles at Delphi. With precision empiricism and rationalism, Godwin identifies the oracular operation as a natural gas-induced fever dream, dressed with various theatricals, and filtered entirely through the secretive, exclusionary priestesses. The combined influence of the Oracles' abilities to deceive and the Greeks' penchant to believe such nonsense affected the histories of entire states, societies, and western civilization itself. Events always turn, after all, at the intersection of interests and ideas.

Greece.

Thus obscure and general is our information respecting the Babylonians. But it was far otherwise with the Greeks. Long before the period, when, by their successful resistance to the Persian invasion, they had rendered themselves of paramount importance in the history of the civilised world, they had their poets and annalists, who preserved to future time the memory of their tastes, their manners and superstitions, their strength, and their weakness. Homer in particular had already composed his two great poems, rendering the peculiarities of his countrymen familiar to the latest posterity. The consequence of this is, that the wonderful things of early Greece are even more frequent than the record of its sober facts. As men advance in observation and experience, they are compelled more and more to perceive that all the phenomena of nature are one vast chain of uninterrupted causes and consequences: but to the eye of uninstructed ignorance every thing is astonishing, every thing is unexpected. The remote generations of mankind are in all cases full of prodigies: but it is the fortune of Greece to have preserved its early adventures, so as to render the beginning pages of its history one mass of impossible falsehoods...

Amphion.

The story of Amphion is more perplexing than that

41

of the living Orpheus. Both of them turn in a great degree upon the miraculous effects of music. Amphion was of the royal family of Thebes, and ultimately became ruler of the territory. He is said, by the potency of his lyre, or his skill in the magic art, to have caused the stones to follow him, to arrange themselves in the way he proposed, and without the intervention of a human hand to have raised a wall about his metropolis. It is certainly less difficult to conceive the savage man to be rendered placable, and to conform to the dictates of civilisation, or even wild beasts to be made tame, than to imagine stones to obey the voice and the will of a human being. The example however is not singular; and hereafter we shall find related that Merlin, the British enchanter, by the power of magic caused the rocks of Stonehenge, though of such vast dimensions, to be carried through the air from Ireland to the place where we at present find them.—Homer mentions that Amphion, and his brother Zethus built the walls of Thebes, but does not describe it as having been done by miracle…

Pythagoras.

…He was a profound geometrician…Pythagoras is the first person, who is known to have taught the spherical figure of the earth, and that we have antipodes; and he propagated the doctrine that the earth is a planet, and that the sun is the centre round which the earth and the other planets move, now known by the name of the Copernican system.

To inculcate a pure and a simple mode of subsistence was also an express object of pursuit to Pythagoras. He taught a total abstinence from every thing having had the property of animal life...

One revolution that Pythagoras worked, was that, whereas, immediately before, those who were most conspicuous among the Greeks as instructors of mankind in understanding and virtue, styled themselves sophists, professors of wisdom, this illustrious man desired to be known only by the appellation of a philosopher, a lover of wisdom. The sophists had previously brought their denomination into discredit and reproach, by the arrogance of their pretensions, and the imperious way in which they attempted to lay down the law to the world.

The modesty of this appellation however did not altogether suit with the deep designs of Pythagoras, the ascendancy he resolved to acquire, and the oracular subjection in which he deemed it necessary to hold those who placed themselves under his instruction. This wonderful man set out with making himself a model of the passive and unscrupulous docility which he afterwards required from others. He did not begin to teach till he was forty years of age, and from eighteen to that period he studied in foreign countries, with the resolution to submit to all his teachers enjoined, and to make himself master of their least communicated and most secret wisdom...

When he came forth, he appeared in a long garment of the purest white, with a flowing beard, and a garland upon his head. He is said to have been of the finest symmetrical form, with a majestic carriage, and a grave and awful countenance. He suffered his followers to believe that he was one of the Gods, the Hyperborean Apollo, and is said to have told Abaris that he assumed the human form, that he might the better invite men to an easiness of approach and to confidence in him. What however seems to be agreed in by all his biographers, is that he professed to have already in different ages appeared in the likeness of man: first as Aethalides, the son of Mercury; and, when his father expressed himself ready to invest him with any gift short of immortality, he prayed that, as the human soul is destined successively to dwell in various forms, he might have the privilege in each to remember his former state of being, which was granted him. From, Aethalides he became Euphorbus, who slew Patroclus at the siege of Troy. He then appeared as Hermotimus, then Pyrrhus, a fisherman of Delos, and finally Pythagoras. He said that a period of time was interposed between each transmigration, during which he visited the seat of departed souls; and he professed to relate a part of the wonders he had seen. He is said to have eaten sparingly and in secret, and in all respects to have given himself out for a being not subject to the ordinary laws of nature.

Pythagoras therefore pretended to miraculous endowments. Happening to be on the sea-shore when

certain fishermen drew to land an enormous multitude of fishes, he desired them to allow him to dispose
of the capture, which they consented to, provided he
would name the precise number they had caught. He
did so, and required that they should throw their prize
into the sea again, at the same time paying them the
value of the fish. He tamed a Daunian bear by whis-
pering in his ear, and prevailed on him henceforth
to refrain from the flesh of animals, and to feed on
vegetables. By the same means he induced an ox not
to eat beans, which was a diet specially prohibited
by Pythagoras; and he called down an eagle from his
flight, causing him to sit on his hand, and submit
to be stroked down by the philosopher. In Greece,
when he passed the river Nessus in Macedon, the
stream was heard to salute him with the words "Hail,
Pythagoras!" When Abaris addressed him as one of
the heavenly host, he took the stranger aside, and convinced him that he was under no mistake, by exhibiting to him his thigh of gold: or, according to another
account, he used the same sort of evidence at a certain
time, to satisfy his pupils of his celestial descent. He
is said to have been seen on the same day at Metapon-
tum in Italy, and at Taurominium in Sicily, though
these places are divided by the sea, so that it was conceived that it would cost several days to pass from
one to the other. In one instance he absented himself
from his associates in Italy for a whole year; and when
he appeared again, related that he had passed that
time in the infernal regions, describing likewise the

45

marvellous things he had seen. Diogenes Laertius, speaking of this circumstance affirms however that he remained during this period in a cave, where his mother conveyed to him intelligence and necessaries, and that, when he came once more into light and air, he appeared so emaciated and colourless, that he might well be believed to have come out of Hades...

His discoveries of various propositions in geometry, of the earth as a planet, and of the solar system as now universally recognised, clearly stamp him a genius of the highest order.

Yet this man, thus enlightened and philanthropical, established his system of proceeding upon narrow and exclusive principles, and conducted it by methods of artifice, quackery and delusion. One of his leading maxims was, that the great and fundamental truths to the establishment of which he devoted himself, were studiously to be concealed from the vulgar, and only to be imparted to a select few, and after years of the severest noviciate and trial. He learned his earliest lessons of wisdom in Egypt after this method, and he conformed through life to the example which had thus been delivered to him. The severe examination that he made of the candidates previously to their being admitted into his school, and the years of silence that were then prescribed to them, testify this. He instructed them by symbols, obscure and enigmatical propositions, which they were first to exercise their ingenuity to expound. The authority and dogmatical assertions of the master were to remain unquestioned;

and the pupils were to fashion themselves to obse-
quious and implicit submission, and were the furthest
in the world from being encouraged to the independent exercise of their own understandings. There was
nothing that Pythagoras was more fixed to discoun-
tenance, than the communication of the truths upon
which he placed the highest value, to the uninitiated.
It is not probable therefore that he wrote any thing:
all was communicated orally, by such gradations, and
with such discretion, as he might think fit to adopt
and to exercise...

He was probably much under the influence of a
contemptible jealousy, and must be considered as
desirous that none of his contemporaries or followers
should eclipse their master. All was oracular and dog-
matic in the school of Pythagoras. He prized and justly
prized the greatness of his attainments and discoveries, and had no conception that any thing could go
beyond them. He did not encourage, nay, he resolutely opposed, all true independence of mind, and
that undaunted spirit of enterprise which is the atmosphere in which the sublimest thoughts are most naturally generated. He therefore did not throw open the
gates of science and wisdom, and invite every comer;
but on the contrary narrowed the entrance, and carefully reduced the number of aspirants. He thought not
of the most likely methods to give strength and per-
manence and an extensive sphere to the progress of
the human mind. For these reasons he wrote nothing;
but consigned all to the frail and uncertain custody

of tradition. And distant posterity has amply avenged itself upon the narrowness of his policy; and the name of Pythagoras, which would otherwise have been ranked with the first luminaries of mankind, and consigned to everlasting gratitude, has in consequence of a few radical and fatal mistakes, been often loaded with obloquy, and the hero who bore it been indiscriminately classed among the votaries of imposture and artifice.

Epimenides.

Epimenides has been mentioned among the disciples of Pythagoras; but he probably lived at an earlier period. He was a native of Crete...

Epimenides appears to have been one of those persons, who make it their whole study to delude their fellow-men, and to obtain for themselves the reputation of possessing supernatural gifts. Such persons, almost universally, and particularly in ages of ignorance and wonder, become themselves the dupes of their own pretensions. He gave out that he was secretly subsisted by food brought to him by the nymphs; and he is said to have taken nourishment in so small quantities, as to be exempted from the ordinary necessities of nature. He boasted that he could send his soul out of his body, and recal it, when he pleased; and alternately appeared an inanimate corpse, and then again his life would return to him, and he appear capable of every human function as before.

He is said to have practised the ceremony of exorcising houses and fields, and thus rendering them fruitful and blessed. He frequently uttered prophecies of events with such forms of ceremony and such sagacious judgment, that they seemed to come to pass as he predicted...

Oracles.

One of the most extraordinary things to be met with in the history of ancient times is the oracles. They maintained their reputation for many successive centuries. The most famous perhaps were that of Delphi in Greece, and that of Jupiter Ammon in the deserts of Lybia. But they were scattered through many cities, many plains, and many islands. They were consulted by the foolish and the wise; and scarcely anything considerable was undertaken, especially about the time of the Persian invasion into Greece, without the parties having first had recourse to these; and they in most cases modified the conduct of princes and armies accordingly. To render the delusion more successful, every kind of artifice was put in practice. The oracle could only be consulted on fixed days; and the persons who resorted to it, prefaced their application with costly offerings to the presiding God. Their questions passed through the hands of certain priests, residing in and about the temple. These priests received the embassy with all due solemnity, and retired. A priestess, or Pythia, who was seldom or never seen by any of the profane vulgar, was the immediate vehicle of communication with the God. She was cut off from all intercourse with the world, and was carefully trained by the attendant priests. Spending almost the whole of her time in solitude, and taught to consider her office as ineffably sacred, she saw visions, and was for the most part in a state of great excitement. The Pythia, at least of the Delphian God, was led on with much ceremony to the performance of her office, and placed upon the sacred tripod. The tripod, we are told, stood over a chasm in the rock, from which issued fumes of an inebriating quality. The Pythia became gradually penetrated through every limb with these fumes, till her bosom swelled, her features enlarged, her mouth foamed, her voice seemed supernatural, and she uttered words that could sometimes scarcely be called articulate. She could with difficulty contain herself, and seemed to be possessed, and wholly overpowered, with the God. After a prelude of many unintelligible sounds, uttered with fervour and a sort of frenzy, she became by degrees more distinct. She uttered incoherent sentences, with breaks and pauses, that were filled up with preternatural efforts and distorted gestures; while the priests stood by, carefully recording her words, and then reducing them into a sort of obscure signification. They finally digested them for the most part into a species of hexameter verse. We may suppose the supplicants during this ceremony placed at a proper distance, so as to observe these things imperfectly, while the less they under-

50

stood, they were ordinarily the more impressed with religious awe, and prepared implicitly to receive what was communicated to them. Sometimes the priestess found herself in a frame, not entirely equal to her function, and refused for the present to proceed with the ceremony.

The priests of the oracle doubtless conducted them in a certain degree like the gipsies and fortune-tellers of modern times, cunningly procuring to themselves intelligence in whatever way they could, and ingeniously worming out the secrets of their suitors, at the same time contriving that their drift should least of all be suspected. But their main resource probably was in the obscurity, almost amounting to unintelligibleness, of their responses. Their prophecies in most cases required the comment of the event to make them understood; and it not seldom happened, that the meaning in the sequel was found to be the diametrically opposite of that which the pious votaries had originally conceived.

In the mean time the obscurity of the oracles was of inexpressible service to the cause of superstition. If the event turned out to be such as could in no way be twisted to come within the scope of the response, the pious suitor only concluded that the failure was owing to the grossness and carnality of his own apprehension, and not to any deficiency in the institution. Thus the oracle by no means lost credit, even when its meaning remained for ever in its original obscurity. But, when, by any fortunate chance, its predictions

51

seemed to be verified, then the unerringness of the oracle was lauded from nation to nation; and the omniscience of the God was admitted with astonishment and adoration...

4

Liars and Legends in Ancient Rome

Godwin shifts from ancient Greece to ancient Rome. The eighth century BCE remains famous in both contexts—for Greece, it was the period in which the *polis* proliferated and replaced Dark Age kings; for Rome, it was the traditional era of her foundation by Romulus and Remus. Then, Rome existed at the fringes of the civilized world, barely over the edge of barbarism. The ignorant early Romans stood in religious *and* civic awe of their new kings. Legend held that Romulus was swept by a spontaneous storm into the heavens. Following such an unexpected turn of events, an influential senator assured the populace that their king had been summoned to live amongst the gods. Rome's second king, Numa, built upon Romulus' elaborate example in showmanship by disappearing into a cave to commune with the goddess Egeria. He emerged from the caves with new legal codes and institutional arrangements that his subjects accepted as the divine will. Not quite so lucky in his attempts at political performance art, Tullus Hostilius attempted to conjure the god Jupiter Elicius, but invoked the god's lightening against himself. He died in a house fire, the *true* causes of which, one can only guess.

In his discussion of the Christian era in Roman history, our author juxtaposes the spiritual magic of the apostles and even Christ himself to the more physical and sensational magic of the pagans. Though Jesus clearly claimed the ability to cast out demons, the career of Simon Magus, for example, is far more *magical*. Yes, yes, Jesus may have offered the only *real* salvation from sin, Godwin hints, but Magus could reportedly *fly through the air*, pass through *miles* of matter at a time, make himself *invisible*; he could *shapeshift*, transfigure matter, bring statues to life, and bid defiance to all locks. He was also—and I stress—*apparently* fire-proof. Not all proper magicians of the period were simple fraudsters, however, nor idealistic carpenters, for that matter. Apollonius of Tyana was a rough contemporary of Jesus born in Asia Minor. After spending years in the Pythagorean cult, he researched a trail across the world, all the way to India. He learned everything he could about the variety of magical traditions each culture offered, eventually synthesizing his knowledge into good deeds for the people of Tyana. Whether magician or mere philosopher, the word "fraudster" simply does not fit well with such a beneficent figure. In fact, as the odd case of the writer Apuleius shows, the individual often has little to do with their own legend. In Apuleius' case, his transcendental literature was mistaken for literal, *magical* manipulations of Nature. Godwin corrects the record, rescuing Apuleius from the condemnation of the ages.

Rome.

Romulus.

The early history of Rome is, as might be expected, interspersed with prodigies. Romulus himself, the founder, after a prosperous reign of many years, disappeared at last by a miracle. The king assembled his army to a general review, when suddenly, in the midst of the ceremony, a tempest arose, with vivid lightnings and tremendous crashes of thunder. Romulus became enveloped in a cloud, and, when, shortly after, a clear sky and serene heavens succeeded, the king was no more seen, and the throne upon which he had sat appeared vacant. The people were somewhat dissatisfied with the event, and appear to have suspected foul play. But the next day Julius Proculus, a senator of the highest character, shewed himself in the general assembly, and assured them, that, with the first dawn of the morning, Romulus had stood before him, and certified to him that the Gods had taken him up to their celestial abodes, authorising him withal to declare to his citizens, that their arms should be for ever successful against all their enemies.

Numa.

Numa was the second king of Rome: and, the object of Romulus having been to render his people soldiers and invincible in war, Numa, an old man and a philosopher, made it his purpose to civilise them, and deeply to imbue them with sentiments of religion. He appears to have imagined the thing best calculated to accomplish this purpose, was to lead them by prodigies and the persuasion of an intercourse with the invisible world. A shield fell from heaven in his time, which he caused to be carefully kept and consecrated to the Gods; and he conceived no means so likely to be effectual to this end, as to make eleven other shields exactly like the one which had descended by miracle, so that, if an accident happened to any one, the Romans might believe that the one given to them by the divinity was still in their possession.

Numa gave to his people civil statutes, and a code of observances in matters of religion; and these also were inforced with a divine sanction. Numa met the goddess Egeria from time to time in a cave; and by her was instructed in the institutions he should give to the Romans: and this barbarous people, awed by the venerable appearance of their king, by the sanctity of his manners, and still more by the divine favour which was so signally imparted to him, received his mandates with exemplary reverence, and ever after implicitly conformed themselves to all that he had suggested.

Tullus Hostilius.

Tullus Hostilius, the third king of Rome, restored again the policy of Romulus. In his time, Alba, the parent state, was subdued and united to its more flourishing colony. In the mean time Tullus, who during the greater part of his reign had been distinguished by martial achievements, in the latter part became the victim of superstitions. A shower of stones fell from heaven, in the manner, as Livy tells us, of a hail-storm. A plague speedily succeeded to this prodigy. Tullus, awed by these events, gave his whole attention to the rites of religion. Among other things he found in the sacred books of Numa an account of a certain ceremony, by which, if rightly performed, the appearance of a God, named Jupiter Elicius, would be conjured up. But Tullus, who had spent his best days in the ensanguined field, proved inadequate to this new undertaking. Some defects having occurred in his performance of the magical ceremony, not only no God appeared at his bidding, but, the anger of heaven being awakened, a thunderbolt fell on the palace, and

the king, and the place of his abode were consumed
together...

Casting Out Devils.

We are now brought down to the era of the Christian
religion; and there is repeated mention of sorcery in
the books of the New Testament.

One of the most frequent miracles recorded of Jesus
Christ is called the "casting out devils." The Pharisees
in the Evangelist, for the purpose of depreciating this
evidence of his divine mission, are recorded to have
said, "this fellow doth not cast out devils, but by
Beelzebub, the prince of devils." Jesus, among other
remarks in refutation of this opprobrium, rejoins upon
them, "If I by Beelzebub cast out devils, by whom
do your children cast them out?" Here then we have
a plain insinuation of sorcery from the lips of Christ
himself, at the same time that he appears to admit that
his adversaries produced supernatural achievements
similar to his own.

Simon Magus.

But the most remarkable passage in the New Testament on the subject of sorcery, is one which describes
the proceedings of Simon Magus, as follows.

"Then Philip went down to the city of Samaria, and
preached Christ unto them. But there was a certain
man, called Simon, which before time in the same city

used sorcery, and bewitched the people of Samaria, giving out that himself was some great one. To whom they all gave heed, from the least to the greatest, saying, 'This man is the great power of God.' And to him they had regard, because that of long time he had bewitched them with sorceries. But, when they believed Philip, preaching the things concerning the kingdom of God and the name of Jesus Christ, they were baptized both men and women. Then Simon himself believed also. And, when he was baptized, he continued with Philip, and wondered, beholding the miracles and signs which were done.

"Now, when the apostles which were at Jerusalem heard that Samaria had received the word of God, they sent unto them Peter and John. Who, when they were come down, prayed for them, that they might receive the Holy Ghost. For as yet he was fallen upon none of them: only they were baptized in the name of the Lord Jesus. Then laid they their hands on them, and they received the Holy Ghost.

"And, when Simon saw that, through the laying on of the apostles' hands, the Holy Ghost was given, he offered them money, saying, Give me also this power, that on whomsoever I lay hands he may receive the Holy Ghost. But Peter said unto him, 'Thy money perish with thee! because thou hast thought that the gift of God might be purchased with money. Thou hast neither part nor lot in this matter: for thy heart is not right in the sight of God. Repent therefore of this thy wickedness, and pray God, if perhaps the thought of thy heart may be forgiven thee: for I perceive that thou art in the gall of bitterness, and in the bond of iniquity.' Then answered Simon, and said, 'Pray ye to the Lord for me, that none of these things which ye have spoken come upon me.'"

This passage of the New Testament leaves us in considerable uncertainty as to the nature of the sorceries, by which "of a long time Simon had bewitched the people of Samaria." But the fathers of the church, Clemens Romanus and Anastasius Sinaita, have presented us with a detail of the wonders he actually performed. When and to whom he pleased he made himself invisible; he created a man out of air; he passed through rocks and mountains without encountering an obstacle; he threw himself from a precipice uninjured; he flew along in the air; he flung himself in the fire without being burned. Bolts and chains were impotent to detain him. He animated statues, so that they appeared to every beholder to be men and women; he made all the furniture of the house and the table to change places as required, without a visible mover; he metamorphosed his countenance and visage into that of another person; he could make himself into a sheep, or a goat, or a serpent; he walked through the streets attended with a multitude of strange figures, which he affirmed to be the souls of the departed; he made trees and branches of trees suddenly to spring up where he pleased; he set up and deposed kings at will; he caused a sickle to go into a field of corn, which unassisted would mow twice as fast as the most industrious reaper.

Thus endowed, it is difficult to imagine what he thought he would have gained by purchasing from the apostles their gift of working miracles. But Clemens Romanus informs us that he complained that, in his sorceries, he was obliged to employ tedious ceremonies and incantations; whereas the apostles appeared to effect their wonders without difficulty and effort, by barely speaking a word.

Elymas, the Sorcerer.

But Simon Magus is not the only magician spoken of in the New Testament. When the apostle Paul came to Paphos in the isle of Cyprus, he found the Roman governor divided in his preference between Paul and Elymas, the sorcerer, who before the governor withstood Paul to his face. Then Paul, prompted by his indignation, said, "Oh, full of all subtlety and mischief, child of the devil, enemy of all righteousness, wilt thou not cease to pervert the right ways of the Lord? And now, behold, the hand of the Lord is upon thee, and thou shalt be blind, not seeing the sun for a season." What wonders Elymas effected to deceive the Roman governor we are not told: but "immediately there fell on him a mist and a darkness; and he went about, seeking some to lead him by the hand."

In another instance we find certain vagabond Jews, exorcists, who pretended to cast out devils from the possessed. But they came to the apostle, and "confessed, and shewed their deeds. Many of them also which used curious arts, brought their books together, and burned them before all. And they counted the price of them, and found it fifty thousand pieces of silver."

It is easy to see however on which side the victory lay. The apostles by their devotion and the integrity of their proceedings triumphed; while those whose only motive was selfishness, the applause of the vulgar, or the admiration of the superficial, gained the honours of a day, and were then swept away into the gulf of general oblivion.

Nero.

The arts of the magician are said to have been called into action by Nero upon occasion of the assassination of his mother, Agrippina. He was visited with occasional fits of the deepest remorse in the recollection of his enormity. Notwithstanding all the ostentatious applauses and congratulations which he obtained from the senate, the army and the people, he complained that he was perpetually haunted with the ghost of his mother, and pursued by the furies with flaming torches and whips. He therefore caused himself to be attended by magicians, who employed their arts to conjure up the shade of Agrippina, and to endeavour to obtain her forgiveness for the crime perpetrated by her son. We are not informed of the success of their evocations...

Apollonius of Tyana.

Apollonius of Tyana in Asia Minor was born nearly at the same time as Jesus Christ, and acquired great reputation while he lived, and for a considerable time after. He was born of wealthy parents, and seems early to have betrayed a passion for philosophy. His father, perceiving this, placed him at fourteen years of age under Euthydemus, a rhetorician of Tarsus; but the youth speedily became dissatisfied with the indolence and luxury of the citizens, and removed himself to Aegas, a neighbouring town, where was a temple of Aesculapius, and where the God was supposed sometimes to appear in person. Here he became professedly a disciple of the sect of Pythagoras. He refrained from animal food, and subsisted entirely on fruits and herbs. He went barefoot, and wore no article of clothing made from the skins of animals. He further imposed on himself a noviciate of five years silence. At the death of his father, he divided his patrimony equally with his brother; and, that brother having wasted his estate by prodigality, he again made an equal division with him of what remained. He travelled to Babylon and Susa in pursuit of knowledge, and even among the Brachmans of India, and appears particularly to have addicted himself to the study of magic. He was of a beautiful countenance and a commanding figure, and, by means of these things, combined with great knowledge, a composed and striking carriage, and much natural eloquence, appears to have won universal favour wherever he went. He is said to have professed the understanding of all languages without learning them, to read the thoughts of men, and to be able to interpret the language of animals. A power of working miracles attended him in all places...

One of the miracles of Apollonius consisted in raising the dead. A young woman of beautiful person was laid out upon a bier, and was in the act of being conveyed to the tomb. She was followed by a multitude of friends, weeping and lamenting, and among others by a young man, to whom she had been on the point to be married. Apollonius met the procession, and commanded those who bore it, to set down the bier. He exhorted the proposed bridegroom to dry up his tears. He enquired the name of the deceased, and, saluting her accordingly, took hold of her hand, and murmured over her certain mystical words. At this act the maiden raised herself on her seat, and presently returned home, whole and sound, to the house of her father...

Divine honours were paid to this philosopher, both during his life, and after his death. The inhabitants of Tyana built a temple to him, and his image was to be found in many other temples. The emperor Adrian collected his letters, and treated them as an invaluable relic. Alexander Severus placed his statue in his oratory, together with those of Jesus Christ, Abraham and

Orpheus, to whom he was accustomed daily to perform the ceremonies of religion...

The publicity of Apollonius and his miracles has become considerably greater, from the circumstance of the early enemies of the Christian religion having instituted a comparison between the miracles of Christ and of this celebrated philosopher, for the obvious purpose of undermining one of the most considerable evidences of the truth of divine revelation. It was probably with an indirect view of this sort that Philostratus was incited by the empress Julia to compose his life of this philosopher; and Hierocles, a writer of the time of Dioclesian, appears to have penned an express treatise in the way of a parallel between the two, attempting to shew a decisive superiority in the miracles of Apollonius.

Apuleius.

Apuleius of Madaura in Africa, who lived in the time of the Antonines, appears to have been more remarkable as an author, than for any thing that occurs in the history of his life. St. Augustine and Lactantius however have coupled him with Apollonius of Tyana, as one of those who for their pretended miracles were brought into competition with the author of the Christian religion. But this seems to have arisen from their misapprehension respecting his principal work, the Golden Ass, which is a romance detailing certain wonderful transformations, and which they appear to have thought was intended as an actual history of the life of the author.

The work however deserves to be cited in this place, as giving a curious representation of the ideas which were then prevalent on the subjects of magic and witchcraft. The author in the course of his narrative says: "When the day began to dawn, I chanced to awake, and became desirous to know and see some marvellous and strange things, remembering that I was now in the midst of Thessaly, where, by the common report of the world, sorceries and enchantments are most frequent. I viewed the situation of the place in which I was; nor was there any thing I saw, that I believed to be the same thing which it appeared. Insomuch that the very stones in the street I thought were men bewitched and turned into that figure, and the birds I heard chirping, the trees without the walls, and the running waters, were changed from human creatures into the appearances they wore. I persuaded myself that the statues and buildings could move, that the oxen and other brute beasts could speak and tell strange tidings, and that I should see and hear oracles from heaven, conveyed on the beams of the sun."

5

Magic and Mysticism in the "East" from Zoroaster to "Arabian Nights"

Temporarily dispensing with the Christianized West, Godwin takes us through the somewhat hidden history of the famous Zoroastrian Magi. The Magi claimed the power to influence natural phenomenon and produce miracles. Godwin notes that easterners, whether Magi *yogis* or independent practitioners, were especially skilled at their craft. Rocail seems to have invented a mechanical automaton disguised as a magically living statue. Hakem acquired fame and infamy through the use of luminescence—probably chemical—supposedly serving to hide his ugliness as well as dazzle and bewilder commoners into a state of deference. Godwin's "Story of a Goule" seems to suggest that a husband took advantage of occultist beliefs to dispose of a troublesome wife.

Each of these stories and the many more which have existed throughout the history of eastern civilizations are most noteworthy to Godwin, however, for their consistency with western myths. Eastern priests and magicians were little different from the westerners—they practiced transfiguration to mystify audiences with visual fantasies; they built intricate fooling machines to convince marks of their supernatural authority; they produced convenient sorcerous excuses for distasteful personal behavior. Regardless of one's culture, necromancy, alchemy, sorcery, and magical showmanship of all kinds provided clever and remorseless individuals a host of socio-political and economic advantages.Our author concludes by speculating that mystical beliefs serve very particular and powerful *functions* for human beings. The particular details of how individuals across cultures utilize mysticism vary, but within the sociological functions of the beliefs lay timeless truths about both the necromancers *and* their societies.

Revolution Produced in the History of
Necromancy and Witchcraft upon the
Establishment of Christianity.

It is necessary here to take notice of the great revolution that took place under Constantine, nearly three hundred years after the death of Christ, when Christianity became the established religion of the Roman empire. This was a period which produced a new era in the history of necromancy and witchcraft. Under the reign of polytheism, devotion was wholly unrestrained in every direction it might chance to assume. Gods known and unknown, the spirits of departed heroes, the Gods of heaven and hell, abstractions of virtue or vice, might unblamed be made the objects of religious worship. Witchcraft therefore, and the invocation of the spirits of the dead, might be practised with toleration; or at all events were not regarded otherwise than as venial deviations from the religion of the state.

It is true, there must always have been a horror of secret arts, especially of such as were of a maleficent nature. At all times men dreaded the mysterious power of spells and incantations, of potent herbs and nameless rites, which were able to control the eternal order of the planets, and the voluntary operations of mind, which could extinguish or recal life, inflame the passions of the soul, blast the works of creation, and extort from invisible beings and the dead the secrets of futurity. But under the creed of the unity of the

69

divine nature the case was exceedingly different. Idolatry, and the worship of other Gods than one, were held to be crimes worthy of the utmost abhorrence and the severest punishment. There was no medium between the worship of heaven and hell. All adoration was to be directed to God the Creator through the mediation of his only begotten Son; or, if prayers were addressed to inferior beings, and the glorified spirits of his saints, at least they terminated in the Most High, were a deprecation of his wrath, a soliciting his favour, and a homage to his omnipotence. On the other hand sorcery and witchcraft were sins of the blackest dye. In opposition to the one only God, the creator of heaven and earth, was the "prince of darkness," the "prince of the power of the air," who contended perpetually against the Almighty, and sought to seduce his creatures and his subjects from their due allegiance. Sorcerers and witches were supposed to do homage and sell themselves to the devil, than which it was not in the mind of man to conceive a greater enormity, or a crime more worthy to cause its perpetrators to be exterminated from the face of the earth. The thought of it was of power to cause the flesh of man to creep and tingle with horror: and such as were prone to indulge their imaginations to the utmost extent of the terrible, found a perverse delight in conceiving this depravity, and were but too much disposed to fasten it upon their fellow-creatures...

History of Necromancy in the East.

From the countries best known in what is usually styled ancient history, in other words from Greece and Rome, and the regions into which the spirit of conquest led the people of Rome and Greece, it is time we should turn to the East, and those remoter divisions of the world, which to them were comparatively unknown.

With what has been called the religion of the Magi, of Egypt, Persia and Chaldea, they were indeed superficially acquainted; but for a more familiar and accurate knowledge of the East we are chiefly indebted to certain events of modern history; to the conquests of the Saracens, when they possessed themselves of the North of Africa, made themselves masters of Spain, and threatened in their victorious career to subject France to their standard; to the crusades; to the spirit of nautical discovery which broke out in the close of the fifteenth century; and more recently to the extensive conquests and mighty augmentation of territory which have been realised by the English East India Company.

The religion of Persia was that of Zoroaster and the Magi. When Ardshir, or Artaxerxes, the founder of the race of the Sassanides, restored the throne of Persia in the year of Christ 226, he called together an assembly of the Magi from all parts of his dominions, and they are said to have met to the number of eighty thousand. These priests, from a remote antiquity, had

71

to a great degree preserved their popularity, and had remarkably adhered to their ancient institutions.

They seem at all times to have laid claim to the power of suspending the course of nature, and producing miraculous phenomena. But in so numerous a body there must have been some whose pretensions were of a more moderate nature, and others who displayed a loftier aspiration. The more ambitious we find designated in their native language by the name of Jogees...

General Silence of the East Respecting Individual Necromancers.

Asia has been more notorious than perhaps any other division of the globe for the vast multiplicity and variety of its narratives of sorcery and magic. I have however been much disappointed in the thing I looked for in the first place, and that is, in the individual adventures of such persons as might be supposed to have gained a high degree of credit and reputation for their skill in exploits of magic. Where the professors are many (and they have been perhaps no where so numerous as those of magic in the East), it is unavoidable but that some should have been more dextrous than others, more eminently gifted by nature, more enthusiastic and persevering in the prosecution of their purpose, and more fortunate in awakening popularity and admiration among their contemporaries. In the instances of Apollonius Tyanaeus and others

among the ancients, and of Cornelius Agrippa, Roger
Bacon and Faust among the moderns, we are
acquainted with many biographical particulars of their
lives, and can trace with some degree of accuracy,
their peculiarities of disposition, and observe how they
were led gradually from one study and one mode of
action to another. But the magicians of the East, so to
speak, are mere abstractions, not characterised by any
of those habits which distinguish one individual of the
human race from another, and having those marking
traits and petty lineaments which make the person, as
it were, start up into life while he passes before our
eyes. They are merely reported to us as men prone to
the producing great signs and wonders, and nothing
more.

Two of the most remarkable exceptions that I have
found to this rule, occur in the examples of Rocail, and
of Hakem, otherwise called Mocanna.

Rocail.

The first of these however is scarcely to be called an
exception, as lying beyond the limits of all credible
history, Rocail is said to have been the younger
brother of Seth, the son of Adam. A Dive, or giant of
mount Caucasus, being hard pressed by his enemies,
sought as usual among the sons of men for aid that
might extricate him out of his difficulties. He at length
made an alliance with Rocail, by whose assistance he
arrived at the tranquillity he desired, and who in con-

sequence became his grand vizier, or prime minister. He governed the dominions of his principal for many years with great honour and success; but, ultimately perceiving the approaches of old age and death, he conceived a desire to leave behind him a monument worthy of his achievements in policy and war. He according erected, we are not told by what means, a magnificent palace, and a sepulchre equally worthy of admiration. But what was most entitled to notice, he peopled this palace with statues of so extraordinary a quality, that they moved and performed all the functions and offices of living men, so that every one who beheld them would have believed that they were actually informed with souls, whereas in reality all they did was by the power of magic, in consequence of which, though they were in fact no more than inanimate matter, they were enabled to obey the behests, and perform the will, of the persons by whom they were visited.

Hakem, Otherwise Mocanna.

Hakem was a leader in one of the different divisions of the followers of Mahomet. To inspire the greater awe into the minds of his supporters, he pretended that he was the Most High God, the creator of heaven and earth, under one of the different forms by which he has in successive ages become incarnate, and made himself manifest to his creatures. He distinguished himself by the peculiarity of always wearing a thick

and impervious veil, by which, according to his followers, he covered the dazzling splendour of his countenance, which was so great that no mortal could
behold it and live, but that, according to his enemies,
only served to conceal the hideousness of his features,
too monstrously deformed to be contemplated without horror. One of his miracles, which seems the most
to have been insisted on, was that he nightly, for a
considerable space of time, caused an orb, something
like the moon, to rise from a sacred well, which gave
a light scarcely less splendid than the day, that diffused
its beams for many miles around. His followers were
enthusiastically devoted to his service, and he supported his authority unquestioned for a number of
years. At length a more formidable opponent
appeared, and after several battles he became obliged
to shut himself up in a strong fortress. Here however
he was so straitly besieged as to be driven to the last
despair, and, having administered poison to his whole
garrison, he prepared a bath of the most powerful
ingredients, which, when he threw himself into it,
dissolved his frame, even to the very bones, so that
nothing remained of him but a lock of his hair. He
acted thus, with the hope that it would be believed
that he was miraculously taken up into heaven; nor
did this fail to be the effect on the great body of his
adherents...

Story of a Goule.

A story in the Arabian Nights, which merits notice
for its singularity, and as exhibiting a particular example of the credulity of the people of the East, is that
of a man who married a sorceress, without being in
any way conscious of her character in that respect. She
was sufficiently agreeable in her person, and he found
for the most part no reason to be dissatisfied with her.
But he became uneasy at the strangeness of her behaviour, whenever they sat together at meals. The husband provided a sufficient variety of dishes, and was
anxious that his wife should eat and be refreshed. But
she took scarcely any nourishment. He set before her a
plate of rice. From this plate she took somewhat, grain
by grain; but she would taste of no other dish. The
husband remonstrated with her upon her way of eat-
ing, but to no purpose; she still went on the same. He
knew it was impossible for any one to subsist upon
so little as she ate; and his curiosity was roused. One
night, as he lay quietly awake, he perceived his wife
rise very softly, and put on her clothes. He watched,
but made as if he saw nothing. Presently she opened
the door, and went out. He followed her unperceived,
by moonlight, and tracked her into a place of graves.
Here to his astonishment he saw her joined by a
Goule, a sort of wandering demon, which is known
to infest ruinous buildings, and from time to time suddenly rushes out, seizes children and other defence-
less people, strangles, and devours them. Occasionally,

for want of other food, this detested race will resort to churchyards, and, digging up the bodies of the newly-buried, gorge their appetites upon the flesh of these. The husband followed his wife and her supernatural companion, and watched their proceedings. He saw them digging in a new-made grave. They extracted the body of the deceased; and, the Goule cutting it up joint by joint, they feasted voraciously, and, having satisfied their appetites, cast the remainder into the grave again, and covered it up as before. The husband now withdrew unobserved to his bed, and the wife followed presently after. He however conceived a horrible loathing of such a wife; and she discovers that he is acquainted with her dreadful secret. They can no longer live together; and a metamorphosis followed. She turned him into a dog, which by ill usage she drove from her door; and he, aided by a benevolent sorceress, first recovers his natural shape, and then, having changed her into a mare, by perpetual hard usage and ill treatment vents his detestation of the character he had discovered in her.

Arabian Nights.

A compilation of more vigorous imagination and more exhaustless variety than the Arabian Nights, perhaps never existed. Almost every thing that can be conceived of marvellous and terrific is there to be found. When we should apprehend the author or authors to have come to an end of the rich vein in which they expatiate, still new wonders are presented to us in endless succession. Their power of comic exhibition is not less extraordinary than their power of surprising and terrifying. The splendour of their painting is endless; and the mind of the reader is roused and refreshed by shapes and colours for ever new.

Resemblance of the Tales of the East and of Europe.

It is characteristic of this work to exhibit a faithful and particular picture of Eastern manners, customs, and modes of thinking and acting. And yet, now and then, it is curious to observe the coincidence of Oriental imagination with that of antiquity and of the North of Europe, so that it is difficult to conceive the one not to be copied from the other. Perhaps it was so; and perhaps not. Man is every where man, possessed of the same faculties, stimulated by the same passions, deriving pain and pleasure from the same sources, with similar hopes and fears, aspirations and alarms.

In the Third Voyage of Sinbad he arrives at an island were he finds one man, a negro, as tall as a palm-tree, and with a single eye in the middle of his forehead. He takes up the crew, one by one, and selects the fattest as first to be devoured. This is done a second time. At length nine of the boldest seize on a spit, while he lay on his back asleep, and, having heated it red-hot, thrust it into his eye.—This is precisely the story of Ulysses and the Cyclops.

The story of the Little Hunchback, who is choked with a fish-bone, and, after having brought successive individuals into trouble on the suspicion of murdering him, is restored to life again, is nearly the best known of the Arabian Tales. The merry jest of Dan Hew, Monk of Leicester, who "once was hanged, and four times slain," bears a very striking resemblance to this.

A similar resemblance is to be found, only changing the sex of the aggressor, between the well known tale of Patient Grizzel, and that of Cheheristany in the Persian Tales. This lady was a queen of the Gins, who fell in love with the emperor of China, and agrees to marry him upon condition that she shall do what she pleases, and he shall never doubt that what she does is right. She bears him a son, beautiful as the day, and throws him into the fire. She bears him a daughter, and gives her to a white bitch, who runs away with her, and disappears. The emperor goes to war with the Moguls; and the queen utterly destroys the provisions of his army. But the fire was a salamander, and the bitch a fairy, who rear the children in the most admirable manner; and the provisions of the army were poisoned by a traitor, and are in a miraculous manner replaced by such as were wholesome and of the most invigorating qualities.

6

Merlin, Dunstan, and Dark Age Britain

Early medieval Europe was a world flush with supernatural entities and powerful individuals who could access this otherworldly power through highly specialized occultic learning. Angels flitted hither and thither through the skies to influence human affairs, demons haunted every crack and crevice in the earth while God's saints endlessly battled them, witches and sorcerers spun their mysterious spells and practiced their magical crafts for both benevolent and malevolent purposes, and alchemists and necromancers desperately searched for an existence extending well beyond the tragically short confines of a natural lifespan. Fraudsters and fanatics of every sort crowded into European monasteries, feudal courts, and dupe-able villages. They ruthlessly and skillfully exploited the mystical foolishness implanted in medieval minds and some of them became so famous that their legacies survived in popular culture for centuries—even to the present day. In his discussion of Europe's Dark Age depths, Godwin pays particular attention to the stories of Merlin and St. Dunstan, both immensely important in folklore and popular culture.

Merlin lived in post-Roman Britain during the long period of Saxon invasions, and his knowledge and talent for building secured him a position bolstering native fortifications. Merlin—*if he was indeed real*—seems to have propagated the story that he was begat of an angel. Coupled with a keen ability to contrive circumstances which baffled the Scots and Pictish kings, the myth of Merlin as part angel proved a powerful aid in securing him a permanent position of influence. The crowning achievement of his wizarding career, however, was building Stonehenge by levitating and transporting massive slabs of stone through the air from Ireland.

Though he lived several centuries later, St. Dunstan drew upon the same mystical cosmology to advance his personal position as did Merlin. Dunstan benefited from a cloistered life as a studious and self-sacrificing abbot. Dunstan supposedly "mortified" his flesh through a variety of means which induced so much pain as to cause hallucinations. Whether real, imagined, or invented by Dunstan for legend-making purposes, these visions were said to have empowered Dunstan to recognize Satan and purge his presence from Glastonbury. For his heroic efforts, he won great renown and power among the kingly courts.

In Godwin's estimation, then, the stories of Merlin and Dunstan demonstrate that in a world bursting with angels and demons, even a small amount of empirical knowledge and technical skill could carry one a long way toward accumulating power and influence.

Dark Ages of Europe.

...In these ages of ignorance, when but few, and those only the most obvious, laws of nature were acknowledged, every event that was not of almost daily occurrence, was contemplated with more or less of awe and alarm. These men "saw God in clouds, and heard him in the wind." Instead of having regard only to that universal Providence, which acts not by partial impulses, but by general laws, they beheld, as they conceived, the immediate hand of the Creator, or rather, upon most occasions, of some invisible intelligence, sometimes beneficent, but perhaps oftener malignant and capricious, interfering, to baffle the foresight of the sage, to humble the pride of the intelligent, and to place the discernment of the most gifted upon a level with the drivellings of the idiot, and the ravings of the insane.

And, as in events men saw perpetually the supernatural and miraculous, so in their fellow-creatures they continually sought, and therefore frequently imagined that they found, a gifted race, that had command over the elements, held commerce with the invisible world, and could produce the most stupendous and terrific effects. In man, as we now behold him, we can ascertain his nature, the strength and pliability of his limbs, the accuracy of his eye, the extent of his intellectual acquisitions, and the subtlety of his powers of thought, and can therefore in a great measure anticipate what we have to hope or to fear from him. Every thing is regulated by what we call natural means. But, in the times I speak of, all was mysterious: the powers of men were subject to no recognised laws: and therefore nothing that imagination could suggest, exceeded the bounds of credibility. Some men were supposed to be so rarely endowed that "a thousand liveried angels" waited on them invisibly, to execute their behests for the benefit of those they favoured; while, much oftener, the perverse and crookedly disposed, who delighted in mischief, would bring on those to whom, for whatever capricious reason, they were hostile, calamities, which no sagacity could predict, and no merely human power could baffle and resist.

After the tenth century enough of credulity remained, to display in glaring colours the aberrations of the human mind, and to furnish forth tales which will supply abundant matter for the remainder of this volume. But previously to this period, we may be morally sure, reigned most eminently the sabbath of magic and sorcery, when nothing was too wild, and remote from the reality of things, not to meet with an eager welcome, when terror and astonishment united themselves with a nameless delight, and the auditor was alarmed even to a sort of madness, at the same time that he greedily demanded an ever-fresh supply of congenial aliment. The more the known laws of the universe and the natural possibility of things were violated, with the stronger marks of approbation was the tale received: while the dextrous impostor, aware of the temper of his age, and knowing how most completely to blindfold and lead astray his prepared dupes, made a rich harvest of the folly of his contemporaries. But I am wrong to call him an impostor. He imposed upon himself, no less than on the gaping crowd. His discourses, even in the act of being pronounced, won upon his own ear; and the dexterity with which he baffled the observation of others, bewildered his ready sense, and filled him with astonishment at the magnitude of his achievements. The accomplished adventurer was always ready to regard himself rather as a sublime being endowed with great and stupendous attributes, than as a pitiful trickster. He became the God of his own idolatry, and stood astonished, as the witch of Endor in the English Bible is represented to have done, at the success of his incantations.

But all these things are passed away, and are buried in the gulf of oblivion. A thousand tales, each more wonderful than the other, marked the year as it glided away. Every valley had its fairies; and every hill its giants. No solitary dwelling, unpeopled with human inhabitants, was without its ghosts; and no church-yard in the absence of day-light could be crossed with impunity....

It is but a small remnant of these marvellous adventures that has been preserved. The greater part of them are swallowed up in that gulf of oblivion, to which are successively consigned after a brief interval all events as they occur, except so far as their memory is preserved through the medium of writing and records. From the eleventh century commences a stream of historical relation, which since that time never entirely eludes the search of the diligent enquirer. Before this period there occasionally appears an historian or miscellaneous writer: but he seems to start up by chance; the eddy presently closes over him, and all is again impenetrable darkness.

When this succession of writers began, they were unavoidably induced to look back upon the ages that had preceded them, and to collect here and there from tradition any thing that appeared especially worthy of notice. Of course any information they could glean was wild and uncertain, deeply stamped with the credulity and wonder of an ignorant period, and still increasing in marvellousness and absurdity from every hand it passed through, and from every tongue which repeated it.

Merlin.

One of the most extraordinary personages whose story is thus delivered to us, is Merlin. He appears to have been contemporary with the period of the Saxon invasion of Britain in the latter part of the fifth century; but probably the earliest mention of his name by any writer that has come down to us is not previous to the eleventh. We may the less wonder therefore at the incredible things that are reported of him. He is first mentioned in connection with the fortune of Vortigern, who is represented by Geoffrey of Monmouth as at that time king of England. The Romans having withdrawn their legions from this island, the unwarlike Britons found themselves incompetent to repel the invasions of the uncivilised Scots and Picts, and Vortigern perceived no remedy but in inviting the Saxons from the northern continent to his aid. The Saxons successfully repelled the invader; but, having done this, they refused to return home. They determined to settle here, and, having taken various towns, are represented as at length inviting Vortigern and his principal nobility to a feast near Salisbury under pretence of a peace, where they treacherously slew three hundred of the chief men of the island, and threw Vortigern into chains. Here, by way of purchasing the restoration of his liberty, they induced him to order the surrender of London, York, Winchester, and other principal towns. Having lost all his strong holds, he consulted his magicians as to how he was to secure himself from this terrible foe. They advised him to build an impregnable tower, and pointed out the situation where it was to be erected. But so unfortunately did their advice succeed, that all the work that his engineers did in the building one day, the earth swallowed, so that no vestige was to be found on the next. The magicians were consulted again on this fresh calamity; and they told the king that that there was no remedying this disaster, other than by cementing the walls of his edifice with the blood of a human being, who was born of no human father.

Vortigern sent out his emissaries in every direction in search of this victim; and at length by strange good fortune they lighted on Merlin near the town of Caermarthen, who told them that his mother was the daughter of a king, but that she had been got with child of him by a being of an angelic nature, and not a man. No sooner had they received this information, than they seized him, and hurried him away to Vortigern as the victim required. But in presence of the king he baffled the magicians; he told the king that the ground they had chosen for his tower, had underneath it a lake, which being drained, they would find at the bottom two dragons of inextinguishable hostility, that under that form figured the Britons and Saxons, all of which upon the experiment proved to be true.

Vortigern died shortly after, and was succeeded first

by Ambrosius, and then by Uther Pendragon. Merlin was the confident of all these kings. To Uther he exhibited a very criminal sort of compliance. Uther became desperately enamoured of Igerna, wife of the duke of Cornwal, and tried every means to seduce her in vain. Having consulted Merlin, the magician contrived by an extraordinary unguent to metamorphose Uther into the form of the duke. The duke had shut up his wife for safety in a very strong tower; but Uther in his new form gained unsuspected entrance; and the virtuous Igerna received him to her embraces, by means of which he begot Arthur, afterwards the most renowned sovereign of this island. Uther now contrived that the duke, her husband, should be slain in battle, and immediately married the fair Igerna, and made her his queen.

The next exploit of Merlin was with the intent to erect a monument that should last for ever, to the memory of the three hundred British nobles that were massacred by the Saxons. This design produced the extraordinary edifice called Stonehenge. These mighty stones, which by no human power could be placed in the position in which we behold them, had originally been set up in Africa, and afterwards by means unknown were transported to Ireland. Merlin commanded that they should be carried over the sea, and placed where they now are, on Salisbury Plain. The workmen, having received his directions, exerted all their power and skill, but could not move one of them. Merlin, having for some time watched their exertions, at length applied his magic; and to the amazement of every one, the stones spontaneously quitted the situation in which they had been placed, rose to a great height in the air, and then pursued the course which Merlin had prescribed, finally settling themselves in Wiltshire, precisely in the position in which we now find them, and which they will for ever retain....

As six hundred years elapsed between the time of Merlin and the earliest known records of his achievements, it is impossible to pronounce what he really pretended to perform, and how great were the additions which successive reporters have annexed to the wonders of his art, more than the prophet himself perhaps ever dreamed of. In later times, when the historians were the contemporaries of the persons by whom the supposed wonders were achieved, or the persons who have for these causes been celebrated have bequeathed certain literary productions to posterity, we may be able to form some conjecture as to the degree in which the heroes of the tale were deluding or deluded, and may exercise our sagacity in the question by what strange peculiarity of mind adventures which we now hold to be impossible obtained so general belief. But in a case like this of Merlin, who lived in a time so remote from that in which his history is first known to have been recorded, it is impracticable to determine at what time the fiction which was afterwards generally received began to be reported, or whether the person to whom the miracles were imputed ever heard or dreamed of the extraordinary things he is represented as having achieved.

St. Dunstan.

An individual scarcely less famous in the dark ages, and who, like Merlin, lived in confidence with successive kings, was St. Dunstan. He was born and died in the tenth century. It is not a little instructive to employ our attention upon the recorded adventures, and incidents occurring in the lives, of such men, since, though plentifully interspersed with impossible tales, they serve to discover to us the tastes and prepossessions of the times in which these men lived, and the sort of accomplishments which were necessary to their success.

St. Dunstan is said to have been a man of distinguished birth, and to have spent the early years of his life in much licentiousness. He was however doubtless a person of the most extraordinary endowments of nature. Ambition early lighted its fire in his bosom; and he displayed the greatest facility in acquiring any talent or art on which he fixed his attention. His career of profligacy was speedily arrested by a dangerous illness, in which he was given over by his physicians. While he lay apparently at the point of death, an angel was suddenly seen, bringing a medicine to him which effected his instant cure. The saint immediately rose from his bed, and hastened to the nearest church to give God thanks for his recovery. As he passed along, the devil, surrounded with a pack of black dogs, inter-posed himself to obstruct his way. Dunstan however intrepidly brandished a rod that he held in his hand, and his opposers took to flight. When he came to the church, he found the doors closed. But the same angel, who effected his cure, was at hand, and, taking him up softly by the hair of his head, placed him before the high altar, where he performed his devotions with suitable fervour.

That he might expiate the irregularities of his past life, St. Dunstan now secluded himself entirely from the world, and constructed for his habitation a cell in the abbey of Glastonbury, so narrow that he could neither stand upright in it, nor stretch out his limbs in repose. He took scarcely so much sustenance as would support life, and mortified his flesh with frequent cas-tigations.

He did not however pass his time during this seclu-sion in vacuity and indolence. He pursued his studies with the utmost ardour, and made a great proficiency in philosophy, divinity, painting, sculpture and music. Above all, he was an admirable chemist, excelled in manufactures of gold and other metals, and was dis-tinguished by a wonderful skill in the art of magic.

During all these mortifications and the severeness of his industry, he appears to have become a prey to extraordinary visions and imaginations. Among the rest, the devil visited him in his cell, and, thrusting his head in at the window, disturbed the saint with obscene and blasphemous speeches, and the most frightful contortions of the features of his countenance. Dunstan at length, wearied out with his perseverance, seized the red-hot tongs with which he was engaged in some chemical experiment, and, catching the devil by the nose, held him with the utmost firmness, while Satan filled the whole neighbourhood for many miles round with his bellowings. Extraordinary as this may appear, it constitutes one of the most prominent incidents in the life of the saint; and the representations of it were for ever repeated in ancient carvings, and in the illuminations of church-windows...

Edred was an inactive prince, but greatly under the dominion of religious prejudices; and Dunstan, being introduced to him, found him an apt subject for his machinations. Edred first made him abbot of Glastonbury, one of the most powerful ecclesiastical dignities in England, and then treasurer of the kingdom. During the reign of this prince, Dunstan disposed of all ecclesiastical affairs, and even of the treasures of the kingdom, at his pleasure.

But Edred filled the throne only nine years, and was succeeded by Edwy at the early age of seventeen, who is said to have been endowed with every grace of form, and the utmost firmness and intrepidity of spirit. Dunstan immediately conceived a jealousy of these qualities, and took an early opportunity to endeavour to disarm them. Edwy entertained a passion for a princess of the royal house, and even proceeded to marry her, though within the degrees forbidden by the canon law. The rest of the story exhibits a lively picture of the manners of these barbarous times. Odo, archbishop of Canterbury, the obedient tool of Dunstan, on the day of the coronation obtruded himself with his abettor into the private apartment, to which the king had retired with his queen, only accompanied by her mother; and here the ambitious abbot, after loading Edwy with the bitterest reproaches for his shameless sensuality, thrust him back by main force into the hall, where the nobles of the kingdom were still engaged at their banquet.

The spirited young prince conceived a deep resentment of this unworthy treatment, and, seizing an opportunity, called Dunstan to account for malversation in the treasury during the late king's life-time. The priest refused to answer; and the issue was that he was banished the realm.

But he left behind him a faithful and implicit coadjutor in archbishop Odo. This prelate is said actually to have forced his way with a party of soldiers into the palace, and, having seized the queen, barbarously to have seared her cheeks with a red-hot iron, and sent her off a prisoner to Ireland. He then proceeded to institute all the forms of a divorce, to which the unhappy king was obliged to submit. Meanwhile the queen, having recovered her beauty, found means to escape, and, crossing the Channel, hastened to join her husband. But here again the priests manifested the same activity as before. They intercepted the queen in her journey, and by the most cruel means undertook to make her a cripple for life. The princess however sunk under the experiment, and ended her existence and her woes together.

A rebellion was now excited against the sacrilegious Edwy; and the whole north of England, having rebelled, was placed under the dominion of his brother, a boy of thirteen years of age. In the midst of these adventures Dunstan returned from the continent, and fearlessly shewed himself in his native country. His party was every where triumphant; Odo being dead, he was installed archbishop of Canterbury, and Edwy, oppressed with calamity on every side, sunk to an untimely grave.

The rest of the life of Dunstan was passed in comparatively tranquillity. He made and unmade kings as he pleased. Edgar, the successor of Edwy, discovered the happy medium of energy and authority as a sovereign, combined with a disposition to indulge the ambitious policy of the priesthood. He was licentious in his amours, without losing a particle of his ascendancy as a sovereign. He however reigned only a few years; but Dunstan at his death found means to place his eldest son on the throne under his special protection, in defiance of the intrigues of the ambitious Elfrida, the king's second wife, who moved heaven and earth to cause the crown to descend upon her own son, as yet comparatively an infant.

In this narrative we are presented with a lively picture of the means by which ambition climbed to its purposes in the darkness of the tenth century. Dunstan was enriched with all those endowments which might seem in any age to lead to the highest distinction. Yet it would appear to have been in vain that he was thus qualified, if he had not stooped to arts that fell in with the gross prejudices of his contemporaries. He had continual recourse to the aid of miracles. He gave into practices of the most rigorous mortification. He studied, and excelled in, all the learning and arts that were then known. But his main dependence was on the art of magic. The story of his taking the devil by the nose with a pair of red-hot tongs, seems to have been of greater service to him than any other single adventure of his life. In other times he might have succeeded in the schemes of his political ambition by seemly and specious means. But it was necessary for him in the times in which he lived, to proceed with eclat, and in a way that should confound all opposers. The utmost resolution was required to overwhelm those who might otherwise have been prompted to contend against him. Hence it appears that he took a right measure of the understanding of his contemporaries, when he dragged the young king from the scene of his retirement, and brought him back by force into the assembly of the nobles. And the inconceivable barbarity practised to the queen, which would have rendered his name horrible in a more civilised age, was exactly calculated to overwhelm the feelings and subject the understandings of the men among whom he lived. The great quality by which he was distinguished was confidence, a frame of behaviour which shewed that he acted from the fullest conviction, and never doubted that his proceedings had the immediate approbation of heaven.

Papal Sorcerers and Technocrats in Medieval Europe

For the remainder of *Lives of the Necromancers*, our author roots his encyclopedic treatment of all things occult in High medieval and Early Modern Europe, especially Britain. In our current selection, Godwin explains the impact of Western-Islamic contact on European witchcraft and proceeds to survey the long history of papal dabbling in magic. In the crusading era (ca. 1090s-early 1500s), many westerners wholeheartedly embraced the knowledge and technology open to them through sustained networks with the Near, Middle, and Far East. Even a century before the Crusades, "The more curious and inquisitive spirits of Europe," including Pope Silvester II, "by degrees adopted the practice of resorting to Spain for the purpose of enlarging their sphere of observation and knowledge." Godwin's selections on three popes illustrate well a larger shift in his treatment of occultism throughout the book.

Silvester II seems to have studiously learned science and technology in the non-western world and translated his knowledge into a reputation for mystical power. What *appeared* supernatural was in fact *technological* power. Benedict IX supposedly engaged in witchcraft as part of his overall lifestyle of "debauchery," reaping the very *worldly* pleasures of sorcery. Pope Gregory VII, whose pontificate was consumed by the Investiture Crisis, posthumously stood charged by his enemies with a variety of necromantic activities. Interestingly, however, Godwin believes Gregory's relentless pursuit of papal power reflected "genuine enthusiasm," rather than mere huckstering or trickery.

Magic could serve many different social purposes, not all of which were the result of ill-will toward others. The final item relays the Muslim tale of a miraculous tub of water. When a man plunges his face into the water, he is transported to an entirely new life, which he then lives day after day, struggle after struggle, joy after joy, to the end of his days. When the lifetime-long vision abruptly ends, the

protagonist emerges from the water tub mere moments
later.

During the late medieval period, elite and learned Europeans became increasingly aware that knowledge and
technology represented the power to transform the world
according to one's own visions. Through exceeding clev-
erness, ingenuity, inventiveness, scrupulousness, and
mechanical skill, men of cunning and vision were often able
to become men of power—and we all know what they say
about power.

Communication of Europe and the Saracens.

It appears to have been about the close of the tenth
century that the more curious and inquisitive spirits
of Europe first had recourse to the East as a source of
such information and art, as they found most glaringly
deficient among their countrymen. We have seen that
in Persia there was an uninterrupted succession of
professors in the art of magic: and, when the followers of Mahomet by their prowess had gained the superiority over the greater part of Asia, over all that was
known of Africa, and a considerable tract of Europe,
they gradually became awake to the desire of cultivat-
ing the sciences, and in particular of making themselves masters of whatever was most liberal and emi-

nent among the disciples of Zoroaster. To this they added a curiosity respecting Greek learning, especially as it related to medicine and the investigation of the powers of physical nature. Bagdad became an eminent seat of learning; and perhaps, next to Bagdad, Spain under the Saracens, or Moors, was a principal abode for the professors of ingenuity and literature.

Gerbert, Pope Silvester II.

As a consequence of this state of things the more curious men of Europe by degrees adopted the practice of resorting to Spain for the purpose of enlarging their sphere of observation and knowledge. Among others Gerbert is reported to have been the first of the Christian clergy, who strung themselves up to the resolution of mixing with the followers of Mahomet, that they might learn from thence things, the knowledge of which it was impossible for them to obtain at home. This generous adventurer, prompted by an insatiable thirst for information, is said to have secretly withdrawn himself from his monastery of Fleury in Burgundy, and to have spent several years among the Saracens of Cordova. Here he acquired a knowledge of the language and learning of the Arabians, particularly of their astronomy, geometry and arithmetic; and he is understood to have been the first that imparted to the north and west of Europe a knowledge of the Arabic numerals, a science, which at first sight might be despised for its simplicity, but which in its conse-

quences is no inconsiderable instrument in subtilising
the powers of human intellect. He likewise introduced the use of clocks. He is also represented to have
made an extraordinary proficiency in the art of magic;
and among other things is said to have constructed a
brazen head, which would answer when it was spoken to, and oracularly resolve many difficult questions.
The same historian assures us that Gerbert by the art of
necromancy made various discoveries of hidden treasures, and relates in all its circumstances the spectacle of a magic palace he visited underground, with the
multiplied splendours of an Arabian tale, but distinguished by this feature, that, though its magnificence
was dazzling to the sight, it would not abide the test
of feeling, but vanished into air, the moment it was
attempted to be touched.

It happened with Gerbert, as with St. Dunstan, that
he united an aspiring mind and a boundless spirit of
ambition, with the intellectual curiosity which has
already been described. The first step that he made
into public life and the career for which he panted,
consisted in his being named preceptor, first to
Robert, king of France, the son of Hugh Capet, and
next to Otho the Third, emperor of Germany. Hugh
Capet appointed him archbishop of Rheims; but, that
dignity being disputed with him, he retired into Germany, and, becoming eminently a favourite with
Otho the Third, he was by the influence of that prince
raised, first to be archbishop of Ravenna, and after-

101

wards to the papacy by the name of Silvester the Second.

Cardinal Benno, who was an adherent of the antipopes, and for that reason is supposed to have calumniated Gerbert and several of his successors, affirms that he was habitually waited on by demons, that by their aid he obtained the papal crown, and that the devil to whom he had sold himself, faithfully promised him that he should live, till he had celebrated high mass at Jerusalem. This however was merely a juggle of the evil spirit; and Gerbert actually died, shortly after having officially dispensed the sacrament at the church of the Holy Cross in Jerusalem, which is one of the seven districts of the city of Rome. This event occurred in the year 1008.

Benedict the Ninth.

According to the same authority sorcery was at this time extensively practised by some of the highest dignitaries of the church, and five or six popes in succession were notorious for these sacrilegious practices. About the same period the papal chair was at its lowest state of degradation; this dignity was repeatedly exposed for sale; and the reign of Gerbert, a man of consummate abilities and attainments, is almost the only redeeming feature in the century in which he lived. At length the tiara became the purchase of an ambitious family, which had already furnished two popes, in behalf of a boy of twelve years of age, who

reigned by the name of Benedict the Ninth. This
youth, as he grew up, contaminated his rule with
every kind of profligacy and debauchery. But even he,
according to Benno, was a pupil in the school of Silvester, and became no mean proficient in the arts of
sorcery. Among other things he caused the matrons
of Rome by his incantations to follow him in troops
among woods and mountains, being bewitched and
their souls subdued by the irresistible charms of his
magic.

Gregory the Seventh.

Benno presents us with a regular catalogue of the
ecclesiastical sorcerers of this period: Benedict the
Ninth, and Laurence, archbishop of Melfi, (each of
whom, he says, learned the art of Silvester), John XX
and Gregory VI. But his most vehement accusations
are directed against Gregory VII, who, he affirms, was
in the early part of his career, the constant companion
and assistant of these dignitaries in unlawful practices
of this sort.

Gregory VII, whose original name was Hildebrand,
is one of the great champions of the Romish church,
and did more than any other man to establish the law
of the celibacy of the clergy, and to take the patron-
age of ecclesiastical dignities out of the hands of the
laity. He was eminently qualified for this undertaking
by the severity of his manners, and the inflexibility of
his resolution to accomplish whatever he undertook.

His great adversary was Henry the Fourth, emperor of Germany, a young prince of high spirit, and at that time (1075) twenty-four years of age...

Gregory was no doubt a man of extraordinary resources and invincible courage. He did not live to witness the triumph of his policy; but his projects for the exaltation of the church finally met with every success his most sanguine wishes could have aspired to. In addition to all the rest it happened, that the countess Matilda, a princess who in her own right possessed extensive sovereignties in Italy, nearly commensurate with what has since been styled the ecclesiastical state, transferred to the pope in her life-time, and confirmed by her testament, all these territories, thus mainly contributing to render him and his successors so considerable as temporal princes, as since that time they have appeared.

It is, however, as a sorcerer, that Gregory VII (Hildebrand) finds a place in this volume. Benno relates that, coming one day from his Alban villa, he found, just as he was entering the church of the Lateran, that he had left behind him his magical book, which he was accustomed to carry about his person. He immediately sent two trusty servants to fetch it, at the same time threatening them most fearfully if they should attempt to look into the volume. Curiosity however got the better of their fear. They opened the book, and began to read; when presently a number of devils appeared, saying, "We are come to obey your commands, but, if we find ourselves trifled with, we shall certainly fall upon and destroy you." The servants, exceedingly terrified, replied, "Our will is that you should immediately throw down so much of the wall of the city as is now before us." The devils obeyed; and the servants escaped the danger that hung over them. It is further said, that Gregory was so expert in the arts of magic, that he would throw out lightning by shaking his arm, and dart thunder from his sleeve.

But the most conspicuous circumstance in the life of Gregory that has been made the foundation of a charge of necromancy against him, is that, when Rodolph marched against Henry IV, the pope was so confident of his success, as to venture publicly to prophesy, both in speech and in writing, that his adversary should be conquered and perish in this campaign. "Nay," he added, "this prophecy shall be accomplished before St. Peter's day; nor do I desire any longer to be acknowledged for pope, than on the condition that this comes to pass." It is added, that Rodolph, relying on the prediction, six times renewed the battle, in which finally he perished instead of his competitor. But this does not go far enough to substantiate a charge of necromancy. It is further remarked, that Gregory was deep in the pretended science of judicial astrology; and this, without its being necessary to have recourse to the solution of diabolical aid, may sufficiently account for the undoubting certainty with which he counted on the event.

In the mean time this statement is of great importance, as illustrative of the spirit of the times in general, and the character of Gregory in particular. Rodolph, the competitor for the empire, has his mind wrought up to such a pitch by this prophetic assurance, that, five times repulsed, he yet led on his forces a sixth time, and perished the victim of his faith. Nor were his followers less animated than he, and from the same cause. We see also from the same story, that Gregory was not an artful and crafty impostor, but a man spurred on by a genuine enthusiasm. And this indeed is necessary to account for the whole of his conduct. The audacity with which he opposed the claims of Henry, and the unheard-of severity with which he treated him at the fortress of Canosa, are to be referred to the same feature of character. Invincible perseverance, when united with great resources of intellect and a lofty spirit, will enable a man thoroughly to effect, what a person of inferior endowments would not have dared so much as to dream of. And Gregory, like St. Dunstan, achieved incredible things, by skilfully adapting himself to circumstances, and taking advantage of the temper and weakness of his contemporaries...

Virgil.

One of the most curious particulars, and which cannot be omitted in a history of sorcery, is the various achievements in the art of magic which have been

related of the poet Virgil. I bring them in here,
because they cannot be traced further back than the
eleventh or twelfth century. The burial-place of this
illustrious man was at Pausilippo, near Naples; the
Neapolitans had for many centuries cherished a peculiar reverence for his memory; and it has been supposed that the old ballads, and songs of the minstrels
of the north of Italy, first originated this idea respecting him. The vulgar of this city, full of imagination
and poetry, conceived the idea of treating him as
the guardian genius of the place; and, in bodying
forth this conception, they represented him in his life-
time as gifted with supernatural powers, which he
employed in various ways for the advantage of a city
that he so dearly loved. Be this as it will, it appears that
Gervais of Tilbury, chancellor to Otho the Fourth,
emperor of Germany, Helinandus, a Cisterian monk,
and Alexander Neckam, all of whom lived about this
time, first recorded these particulars in their works.

They tell us, that Virgil placed a fly of brass over
one of the gates of the city, which, as long as it continued there, that is, for a space of eight years, had
the virtue of keeping Naples clear from moskitoes and
all noxious insects: that he built a set of shambles,
the meat in which was at all times free from putre-
faction: that he placed two images over the gates of
the city, one of which was named Joyful, and the
other Sad, one of resplendent beauty, and the other
hideous and deformed, and that whoever entered the
town under the former image would succeed in all his

107

undertakings, and under the latter would as certainly miscarry: that he caused a brazen statue to be erected on a mountain near Naples, with a trumpet in his mouth, which when the north wind blew, sounded so shrill as to drive to the sea the fire and smoke which issued from the neighbouring forges of Vulcan: that he built different baths at Naples, specifically prepared for the cure of every disease, which were afterwards demolished by the malice of the physicians: and that he lighted a perpetual fire for the refreshment of all travellers, close to which he placed an archer of brass, with his bow bent, and this inscription, "Whoever strikes me, I will let fly my arrow:" that a foolhardy fellow notwithstanding struck the statue, when the arrow was immediately shot into the fire, and the fire was extinguished. It is added, that, Naples being infested with a vast multitude of contagious leeches, Virgil made a leech of gold, which he threw into a pit, and so delivered the city from the infection: that he surrounded his garden with a wall of air, within which the rain never fell: that he built a bridge of brass that would transport him wherever he pleased: that he made a set of statues, which were named the salvation of Rome, which had the property that, if any one of the subject nations prepared to revolt, the statue, which bore the name of, and was adored by that nation, rung a bell, and pointed with its finger in the direction of the danger: that he made a head, which had the virtue of predicting things future: and lastly, amidst a world of other wonders, that he cut a subterranean passage through mount Pausilippo, that travellers might pass with perfect safety, the mountain having before been so infested with serpents and dragons, that no one could venture to cross it....

Miracle of the Tub of Water.

This story affords an additional example of the affinity between the ancient Asiatic and European legends, so as to convince us that it is nearly impossible that the one should not be in some way borrowed from the other. There is, in a compilation called the Turkish Tales, a story of an infidel sultan of Egypt, who took the liberty before a learned Mahometan doctor, of ridiculing some of the miracles ascribed to the prophet, as for example his transportation into the seventh heaven, and having ninety thousand conferences with God, while in the mean time a pitcher of water, which had been thrown down in the first step of his ascent, was found with the water not all spilled at his return.

The doctor, who had the gift of working miracles, told the sultan that, with his consent, he would give him a practical proof of the possibility of the circumstance related of Mahomet. The sultan agreed. The doctor therefore directed that a huge tub of water should be brought in, and, while the prince stood before it with his courtiers around, the holy man bade him plunge his head into the water, and draw it out again. The sultan immersed his head, and had no sooner done so, than he found himself alone at the foot of a mountain on a desert shore. The prince first began to rave against the doctor for this piece of treachery and witchcraft. Perceiving however that all his rage was vain, and submitting himself to the imperiousness of his situation, he began to seek for some habitable tract. By and by he discovered people cutting down wood in a forest, and, having no remedy, he was glad to have recourse to the same employment. In process of time he was brought to a town; and there by great good fortune, after other adventures, he married a woman of beauty and wealth, and lived long enough with her, for her to bear him seven sons and seven daughters. He was afterwards reduced to want, so as to be obliged to ply in the streets as a porter for his livelihood. One day, as he walked alone on the sea-shore, ruminating on his hard fate, he was seized with a fit of devotion, and threw off his clothes, that he might wash himself, agreeably to the Mahometan custom, previously to saying his prayers. He had no sooner however plunged into the sea, and raised his head again above water, than he found himself standing by the side of the tub that had been brought in, with all the great persons of his court round him, and the holy man close at his side. He found that the long series of imaginary adventures he had passed through, had in reality occupied but one minute of time.

8

Albertus Magnus, Roger Bacon, and the Alchemy Cult

In Europe's High Middle Ages, knowledge of and participation in the occult broadened well beyond the realm of highly-educated popes, secluded monks and traveling hucksters. As Godwin details in our current selection, a seemingly endless array of friars, philosophers, scientists, alchemists, and educators joined the magical fray to advance their own power, influence, and visions.

Unlike their cloistered cousins in the monasteries, friars

lived and preached among the people. The friars "were distinguished by a fervor of devotion," essentially independent of the church hierarchy, and they possessed a distinctly ferocious commitment to charity and science which made them both rare and indispensable to their world. The friars largely divided over time into sects of Dominicans and Franciscans, "and all that was most illustrious in intellect at this period belonged either to the one or the other." These new men of learning who proliferated across a more and more commercially prosperous Europe constructed grand machines like Albertus Magnus' automatons; they discovered powerful and mysterious new substances like Roger Bacon's gunpowder; they supposedly communicated with the Devil, receiving the inspiration for inventions like artificial intelligence; they performed incredible feats of transfiguration on themselves, the bodies of others, and all sorts of physical material; and generations of alchemists tinkered away, either hopelessly attempting to turn lesser metals into gold, struggling to create the elixir of life, or cleverly devising ways to fool royals into giving them more money.

Godwin concludes the section by introducing the reader to the light of Renaissance humanism. With figures like Petrarch, "the energies of the human mind were to loosen its shackles, and its independence was ultimately to extinguish those delusions and that superstition which had so long enslaved it." Through an ironic twist of history, the enlightened and educated no longer *practiced* witchcraft,

but they would have defended to the death your right to
do so.

Communication of Europe and the Saracens.

Institution of Friars.

About this time a great revolution took place in the
state of literature in Europe. The monks, who at one
period considerably contributed to preserve the mon-
uments of ancient learning, memorably fell off in reputation and industry. Their communities by the dona-
tions of the pious grew wealthy; and the monks themselves inhabited splendid palaces, and became luxuri-
ous, dissipated and idle. Upon the ruins of their good
fame rose a very extraordinary race of men, called Friars. The monks professed celibacy, and to have no
individual property; but the friars abjured all property, both private and in common. They had no place
where to lay their heads, and subsisted as mendicants
upon the alms of their contemporaries. They did not
hide themselves in refectories and dormitories, but
lived perpetually before the public. In the sequel
indeed they built Friaries for their residence; but these
were no less distinguished for the simplicity and hum-
bleness of their appearance, than the monasteries were
for their grandeur and almost regal magnificence. The

Friars were incessant in preaching and praying, voluntarily exposed themselves to the severest hardships, and were distinguished by a fervour of devotion and charitable activity that knew no bounds. We might figure them to ourselves as swallowed up in these duties. But they added to their merits an incessant earnestness in learning and science. A new era in intellect and subtlety of mind began with them; and a set of the most wonderful men in depth of application, logical acuteness, and discoveries in science distinguished this period. They were few indeed, in comparison of the world of ignorance that every where surrounded them; but they were for that reason only the more conspicuous. They divided themselves principally into two orders, the Dominicans and Franciscans. And all that was most illustrious in intellect at this period belonged either to the one or the other.

Albertus Magnus.

Albertus Magnus, a Dominican, was one of the most famous of these. He was born according to some accounts in the year 1193, and according to others in 1205. It is reported of him, that he was naturally very dull, and so incapable of instruction, that he was on the point of quitting the cloister from despair of learning what his vocation required, when the blessed virgin appeared to him in a vision, and enquired of him in which he desired to excel, philosophy or divinity. He chose philosophy; and the virgin assured him

114

that he should become incomparable in that, but, as a punishment for not having chosen divinity, he should sink, before he died, into his former stupidity. It is added that, after this apparition, he had an infinite deal of wit, and advanced in science with so rapid a progress as utterly to astonish the masters. He afterwards became bishop of Ratisbon.

It is related of Albertus, that he made an entire man of brass, putting together its limbs under various constellations, and occupying no less than thirty years in its formation. This man would answer all sorts of questions, and was even employed by its maker as a domestic. But what is more extraordinary, this machine is said to have become at length so garrulous, that Thomas Aquinas, being a pupil of Albertus, and finding himself perpetually disturbed in his abstrusest speculations by its uncontrolable loquacity, in a rage caught up a hammer, and beat it to pieces. According to other accounts the man of Albertus Magnus was composed, not of metal, but of flesh and bones like other men; but this being afterwards judged to be impossible, and the virtue of images, rings, and planetary sigils being in great vogue, it was conceived that this figure was formed of brass, and indebted for its virtue to certain conjunctions and aspects of the planets...

Roger Bacon.

Roger Bacon, of whom extraordinary stories of magic

have been told, and who was about twenty years younger than Albertus, was one of the rarest geniuses that have existed on earth. He was a Franciscan friar. He wrote grammars of the Latin, Greek and Hebrew languages. He was profound in the science of optics. He explained the nature of burning-glasses, and of glasses which magnify and diminish, the microscope and the telescope. He discovered the composition of gunpowder. He ascertained the true length of the solar year; and his theory was afterwards brought into general use, but upon a narrow scale, by Pope Gregory XIII, nearly three hundred years after his death.

But for all these discoveries he underwent a series of the most bitter persecutions. It was imputed to him by the superiors of his order that the improvements he suggested in natural philosophy were the effects of magic, and were suggested to him through an intercourse with infernal spirits. They forbade him to communicate any of his speculations. They wasted his frame with rigorous fasting, often restricting him to a diet of bread and water, and prohibited all strangers to have access to him. Yet he went on indefatigably in pursuit of the secrets of nature. At length Clement IV, to whom he appealed, procured him a considerable degree of liberty. But, after the death of that pontiff, he was again put under confinement, and continued in that state for a further period of ten years. He was liberated but a short time before his death.

Freind says, that, among other ingenious contrivances, he put statues in motion, and drew articulate sounds from a brazen head, not however by magic, but by an artificial application of the principles of natural philosophy. This probably furnished a foundation for the tale of Friar Bacon and Friar Bungy, which was one of the earliest productions to which the art of printing was applied in England. These two persons are said to have entertained the project of inclosing England with a wall, so as to render it inaccessible to any invader. They accordingly raised the devil, as the person best able to inform them how this was to be done. The devil advised them to make a brazen head, with all the internal structure and organs of a human head. The construction would cost them much time; and they must then wait with patience till the faculty of speech descended upon it. It would finally however become an oracle, and, if the question were propounded to it, would teach them the solution of their problem. The friars spent seven years in bringing the structure to perfection, and then waited day after day, in expectation that it would utter articulate sounds. At length nature became exhausted in them, and they lay down to sleep, having first given it strictly in charge to a servant of theirs, clownish in nature, but of strict fidelity, that he should awaken them the moment the image began to speak. That period arrived. The head uttered sounds, but such as the clown judged unworthy of notice. "Time is!" it said. No notice was taken; and a long pause ensued. "Time was!" A similar pause, and no notice. "Time is passed!" And the moment these words were uttered, a tremendous storm ensued, with thunder and lightning, and the head was shivered into a thousand pieces. Thus the experiment of friar Bacon and friar Bungy came to nothing...

Peter of Apono.

Peter of Apono, so called from a village of that name in the vicinity of Padua, where he was born in the year 1250, was an eminent philosopher, mathematician and astrologer, but especially excelled in physic. Finding that science at a low ebb in his native country, he resorted to Paris, where it especially flourished; and after a time returning home, exercised his art with extraordinary success, and by this means accumulated great wealth.

But all his fame and attainments were poisoned to him by the accusation of magic. Among other things he was said to possess seven spirits, each of them inclosed in a crystal vessel, from whom he received every information he desired in the seven liberal arts. He was further reported to have had the extraordinary faculty of causing the money he expended in his disbursements, immediately to come back into his own purse. He was besides of a hasty and revengeful temper. In consequence of this it happened to him, that, having a neighbour, who had an admirable spring of water in his garden, and who was accustomed to suffer the physician to send for a daily supply, but who for some displeasure or inconvenience withdrew his permission, Peter d'Apono, by the aid of the devil, removed the spring from the garden in which it had flowed, and turned it to waste in the public street. For some of these accusations he was called to account by the tribunal of the inquisition. While he was upon his trial however, the unfortunate man died. But so unfavourable was the judgment of the inquisitors respecting him, that they decreed that his bones should be dug up, and publicly burned. Some of his friends got intimation of this, and saved him from the impending disgrace by removing his remains. Disappointed in this, the inquisitors proceeded to burn him in effigy...

Ziito.

Very extraordinary things are related of Ziito, a sorcerer, in the court of Wenceslaus, king of Bohemia and afterwards emperor of Germany, in the latter part of the fourteenth century. This is perhaps, all things considered, the most wonderful specimen of magical power any where to be found. It is gravely recorded by Dubravius, bishop of Olmutz, in his History of Bohemia. It was publicly exhibited on occasion of the marriage of Wenceslaus with Sophia, daughter of the elector Palatine of Bavaria, before a vast assembled multitude.

The father-in-law of the king, well aware of the bridegroom's known predilection for theatrical exhibitions and magical illusions, brought with him to

Prague, the capital of Wenceslaus, a whole waggon-load of morrice-dancers and jugglers, who made their appearance among the royal retinue. Meanwhile Ziito, the favourite magician of the king, took his place obscurely among the ordinary spectators. He however immediately arrested the attention of the strangers, being remarked for his extraordinary deformity, and a mouth that stretched completely from ear to ear. Ziito was for some time engaged in quietly observing the tricks and sleights that were exhibited. At length, while the chief magician of the elector Palatine was still busily employed in shewing some of the most admired specimens of his art, the Bohemian, indignant at what appeared to him the bungling exhibitions of his brother-artist, came forward, and reproached him with the unskilfulness of his performances. The two professors presently fell into warm debate. Ziito, provoked at the insolence of his rival, made no more ado but swallowed him whole before the multitude, attired as he was, all but his shoes, which he objected to because they were dirty. He then retired for a short while to a closet, and presently returned, leading the magician along with him.

Having thus disposed of his rival, Ziito proceeded to exhibit the wonders of his art. He shewed himself first in his proper shape, and then in those of different persons successively, with countenances and a stature totally dissimilar to his own; at one time splendidly attired in robes of purple and silk, and then in the twinkling of an eye in coarse linen and a clownish coat of frieze. He would proceed along the field with a smooth and undulating motion without changing the posture of a limb, for all the world as if he were carried along in a ship. He would keep pace with the king's chariot, in a car drawn by barn-door fowls. He also amused the king's guests as they sat at table, by causing, when they stretched out their hands to the different dishes, sometimes their hands to turn into the cloven feet of an ox, and at other times into the hoofs of a horse. He would clap on them the antlers of a deer, so that, when they put their heads out at window to see some sight that was going by, they could by no means draw them back again; while he in the mean time feasted on the savoury cates [delicacies] that had been spread before them, at his leisure.

At one time he pretended to be in want of money, and to task his wits to devise the means to procure it. On such an occasion he took up a handful of grains of corn, and presently gave them the form and appearance of thirty hogs well fatted for the market. He drove these hogs to the residence of one Michael, a rich dealer, but who was remarked for being penurious and thrifty in his bargains. He offered them to Michael for whatever price he should judge reasonable. The bargain was presently struck, Ziito at the same time warning the purchaser, that he should on no account drive them to the river to drink. Michael however paid no attention to this advice; and the hogs no sooner arrived at the river, than they turned into grains of corn as before. The dealer, greatly enraged at this trick, sought high and low for the seller that he might be revenged on him. At length he found him in a vintner's shop seemingly in a gloomy and absent frame of mind, reposing himself, with his legs stretched out on a form. The dealer called out to him, but he seemed not to hear. Finally he seized Ziito by one foot, plucking at it with all his might. The foot came away with the leg and thigh; and Ziito screamed out, apparently in great agony. He seized Michael by the nape of the neck, and dragged him before a judge. Here the two set up their separate complaints, Michael for the fraud that had been committed on him, and Ziito for the irreparable injury he had suffered in his person. From this adventure came the proverb, frequent in the days of the historian, speaking of a person who had made an improvident bargain, "He has made just such a purchase as Michael did with his hogs."

Transmutation of Metals.

Among the different pursuits, which engaged the curiosity of active minds in these unenlightened ages, was that of the transmutation of the more ordinary metals into gold and silver. This art, though not properly of necromantic nature, was however elevated by its professors, by means of an imaginary connection between it and astrology, and even between it and an intercourse with invisible spirits. They believed, that their investigations could not be successfully prosecuted but under favourable aspects of the planets, and

that it was even indispensible to them to obtain supernatural aid.

In proportion as the pursuit of transmutation, and
the search after the elixir of immortality grew into
vogue, the adepts became desirous of investing them
with the venerable garb of antiquity. They endeavoured to carry up the study to the time of Solomon;
and there were not wanting some who imputed it
to the first father of mankind. They were desirous to
track its footsteps in Ancient Egypt; and they found
a mythological representation of it in the expedition
of Jason after the golden fleece, and in the cauldron
by which Medea restored the father of Jason to his
original youth. But, as has already been said, the first
unquestionable mention of the subject is to be referred
to the time of Dioclesian. From that period traces of
the studies of the alchemists from time to time regu-
larly discover themselves.

The study of chemistry and its supposed invaluable
results was assiduously cultivated by Geber and the
Arabians.

Artephius.

Artephius is one of the earliest names that occur
among the students who sought the philosopher's
stone. Of him extraordinary things are told. He lived
about the year 1130, and wrote a book of the Art
of Prolonging Human Life, in which he professes to
have already attained the age of one thousand and

twenty-five years. He must by this account have been born about one hundred years after our Saviour. He professed to have visited the infernal regions, and there to have seen Tantalus seated on a throne of gold. He is also said by some to be the same person, whose life has been written by Philostratus under the name of Apollonius of Tyana. He wrote a book on the philosopher's stone, which was published in Latin and French at Paris in the year 1612.

Raymond Lulli.

Among the European students of these interesting secrets a foremost place is to be assigned to Raymond Lulli and Arnold of Villeneuve.

Lulli was undoubtedly a man endowed in a very eminent degree with the powers of intellect. He was a native of the island of Majorca, and was born in the year 1234. He is said to have passed his early years in profligacy and dissipation, but to have been reclaimed by the accident of falling in love with a young woman afflicted with a cancer. This circumstance induced him to apply himself intently to the study of chemistry and medicine, with a view to discover a cure for her complaint, in which he succeeded. He afterwards entered into the community of Franciscan friars.

Edward the First was one of the most extraordinary princes that ever sat on a throne. He revived the study of the Roman civil law with such success as to have merited the title of the English Justinian. He was no less distinguished as the patron of arts and letters. He invited to England Guido dalla Colonna, the author of the Troy Book, and Raymond Lulli. This latter was believed in his time to have prosecuted his studies with such success as to have discovered the elixir vitae, by means of which he could keep off the assaults of old age, at least for centuries, and the philosopher's stone. He is affirmed by these means to have supplied to Edward the First six millions of money, to enable him to carry on war against the Turks.

But he was not only indefatigable in the pursuit of natural science. He was also seized with an invincible desire to convert the Mahometans to the Christian faith. For this purpose he entered earnestly upon the study of the Oriental languages. He endeavoured to prevail on different princes of Europe to concur in his plan, and to erect colleges for the purpose, but without success. He at length set out alone upon his enterprise, but met with small encouragement. He penetrated into Africa and Asia. He made few converts, and was with difficulty suffered to depart, under a solemn injunction that he should not return. But Lulli chose to obey God rather than man, and ventured a second time. The Mahometans became exasperated with his obstinacy, and are said to have stoned him to death at the age of eighty years. His body was however transported to his native place; and miracles are reported to have been worked at his tomb.

Raymond Lulli is beside famous for what he was

pleased to style his Great Art. The ordinary accounts however that are given of this art assume a style of burlesque, rather than of philosophy. He is said to have boasted that by means of it he could enable any one to argue logically on any subject for a whole day together, independently of any previous study of the subject in debate. To the details of the process Swift seems to have been indebted for one of the humorous projects described by him in his voyage to Laputa. Lulli recommended that certain general terms of logic, metaphysics, ethics or theology should first be collected. These were to be inscribed separately upon square pieces of parchment. They were then to be placed on a frame so constructed that by turning a handle they might revolve freely, and form endless combinations. One term would stand for a subject, and another for a predicate. The student was then diligently to inspect the different combinations that fortuitously arose, and exercising the subtlety of his faculties to select such as he should find best calculated for his purposes. He would thus carry on the process of his debate; and an extraordinary felicity would occasionally arise, suggesting the most ingenious hints, and leading on to the most important discoveries.—If a man with the eminent faculties which Lulli otherwise appeared to have possessed really laid down the rules of such an art, all he intended by it must have been to satirize the gravity with which the learned doctors of his time carried on their grave disputations in mood and figure, having regard only to the severity of the rule by which they debated, and holding themselves totally indifferent whether they made any real advances in the discovery of truth.

English Laws Respecting Transmutation.

So great an alarm was conceived about this time respecting the art of transmutation, that an act of parliament was passed in the fifth year of Henry IV, 1404, which lord Coke states as the shortest of our statutes, determining that the making of gold or silver shall be deemed felony. This law is said to have resulted from the fear at that time entertained by the houses of lords and commons, lest the executive power, finding itself by these means enabled to increase the revenue of the crown to any degree it pleased, should disdain to ask aid from the legislature; and in consequence should degenerate into tyranny and arbitrary power...

Revival of Letters.

While these things were going on in Europe, the period was gradually approaching, when the energies of the human mind were to loosen its shackles, and its independence was ultimately to extinguish those delusions and that superstition which had so long enslaved it. Petrarch, born in the year 1304, was deeply impregnated with a passion for classical lore, was smitten with the love of republican institutions, and especially distinguished himself for an adoration of Homer. Dante, a more sublime and original genius than Petrarch, was his contemporary. About the same time Boccaccio in his *Decamerone* gave at once to Italian prose that purity and grace, which none of his successors in the career of literature have ever been able to excel. And in our own island Chaucer with a daring hand redeemed his native tongue from the disuse and ignominy into which it had fallen, and poured out the immortal strains that the genuine lovers of the English tongue have ever since perused with delight, while those who are discouraged by its apparent crabbedness, have yet grown familiar with his thoughts in the smoother and more modern versification of Dryden and Pope. From that time the principles of true taste have been more or less cultivated, while with equal career independence of thought and an ardent spirit of discovery have continually proceeded, and made a rapid advance towards the perfect day.

But the dawn of literature and intellectual freedom were still a long time ere they produced their full effect. The remnant of the old woman clung to the heart with a tenacious embrace. Three or four centuries elapsed, while yet the belief in sorcery and witchcraft was alive in certain classes of society. And then, as is apt to occur in such cases, the expiring folly occasionally gave tokens of its existence with a convulsive vehemence, and became only the more picturesque and impressive through the strong contrast of lights and shadows that attended its manifestations.

9

Joan of Arc & the Witch Hunters

From this point forward in the volume, William Godwin takes a much more conciliatory and pitying tone toward his subject witches and necromancers. During the Renaissance, Europeans became more and more keenly aware of the physical laws governing natural phenomenon. In the process, they learned a sharp lesson about human credulity and the limits of actual occultic practice. As scientists uncovered the facts of nature, they left firmly behind them the superstitions of early ages. Science helped to demystify witchcraft and expose it as a sociological, not supernatural, phenomenon. Political institutions, however, lagged cutting-edge learning by several centuries and witches continued to suffer at the hands of persecutionists. While the period ca. 1300-1650 witnessed an explosion of scientific and technological learning, Europeans also dug themselves into deep and violently antagonistic religious and political positions. Marginalized and powerless individuals often made easy targets both for angry mobs and political or religious leaders in desperate need of a scapegoat. Among these marginalized groups sacrificed to violent forces in European history were Godwin's necromancers, sorcerers, alchemists, and all the rest. In our current selection, Godwin details the famous story of Joan of Arc followed by a long string of tales from centuries of witch trials, torture, and executions.

Revival of Letters

While these things were going on in Europe, the period was gradually approaching when the engergies of the human mind were to loosen its shackles, and its independence was ultimately to extinguish those delusions and that superstition which had so long enslaved it...

But the dawn of literature and intellectual freedom were still a long time ere they produced their full effect. The remnant of the old woman clung to the heard with a tenacious embrace. Three or four centuries elapsed, while yet the belief in sorcery and witchcraft was alive in certain classes of society. And then, as is apt to occur in such cases, the expiring folly occasionally gave tokens of its existence with a convulsive vehemence, and became only the more picturesque and impressive through the strong contrasts of lights and shadows that attended its manifestations.

Joan of Arc.

One of the most memorable stories on record is that of Joan of Arc, commonly called the Maid of Orleans. Henry the Fifth of England won the decisive battle of Agincourt in the year 1415, and some time after concluded a treaty with the reigning king of France, by which he was recognised, in case of that king's death, as heir to the throne. Henry V died in the year 1422, and Charles VI of France in less than two months after. Henry VI was only nine months old at the time of his father's death; but such was the deplorable state of France, that he was in the same year proclaimed king in Paris, and for some years seemed to have every prospect of a fortunate reign. John, Duke of Bedford, the king's uncle, was declared regent of France: the son of Charles VI was reduced to the last extremity; Orleans was the last strong town in the heart of the kingdom which held out in his favour; and that place seemed on the point to surrender to the conqueror.

In this fearful crisis appeared Joan of Arc, and in the most incredible manner turned the whole tide of affairs. She was a servant in a poor inn at Domremi, and was accustomed to perform the coarsest offices, and in particular to ride the horses to a neighbouring stream to water. Of course the situation of France and her hereditary king formed the universal subject of conversation; and Joan became deeply impressed with the lamentable state of her country and the misfortunes of her king. By dint of perpetual meditation, and feeling in her breast the promptings of energy and enterprise, she conceived the idea that she was destined by heaven to be the deliverer of France. Agreeably to the state of intellectual knowledge at that period, she persuaded herself that she saw visions, and held communication with the saints. She had conversations with St. Margaret, and St. Catherine of Fierbois. They told her that she was commissioned by God to raise the siege of Orleans, and to conduct Charles VII to his coronation at Rheims. St. Catherine commanded her to demand a sword which was in her church at Fierbois, which the Maid described by particular tokens, though she had never seen it. She then presented herself to Baudricourt, governor of the neighbouring town of Vaucouleurs, telling him her commission, and requiring him to send her to the king at Chinon. Baudricourt at first made light of her application; but her importunity and the ardour she expressed at length excited him. He put on her a man's attire, gave her arms, and sent her under an escort of two gentlemen and their attendants to Chinon. Here she immediately addressed the king in person, who

132

had purposely hid himself behind his courtiers that she might not know him. She then delivered her message, and offered in the name of the Most High to raise the siege of Orleans, and conduct king Charles to Rheims to be anointed. As a further confirmation she is said to have revealed to the king before a few select friends, a secret, which nothing but divine inspiration could have discovered to her.

Desperate as was then the state of affairs, Charles and his ministers immediately resolved to seize the occasion that offered, and put forward Joan as an instrument to revive the prostrate courage of his subjects. He had no sooner determined on this, than he pretended to submit the truth of her mission to the most rigorous trial. He called together an assembly of theologians and doctors, who rigorously examined Joan, and pronounced in her favour. He referred the question to the parliament of Poitiers; and they, who met persuaded that she was an impostor, became convinced of her inspiration. She was mounted on a high-bred steed, furnished with a consecrated banner, and marched, escorted by a body of five thousand men, to the relief of Orleans. The French, strongly convinced by so plain an interposition of heaven, resumed the courage to which they had long been strangers. Such a phenomenon was exactly suited to the superstition and credulity of the age. The English were staggered with the rumours that every where went before her, and struck with a degree of apprehension and terror that they could not shake off. The garrison, informed of her approach, made a sally on the other side of the town; and Joan and her convoy entered without opposition. She displayed her standard in the market-place, and was received as a celestial deliverer.

She appears to have been endowed with a prudence, not inferior to her courage and spirit of enterprise. With great docility she caught the hints of the commanders by whom she was surrounded; and, convinced of her own want of experience and skill, delivered them to the forces as the dictates of heaven. Thus the knowledge and discernment of the generals were brought into play, at the same time that their suggestions acquired new weight, when falling from the lips of the heaven-instructed heroine. A second convoy arrived; the waggons and troops passed between the redoubts of the English; while a dead silence and astonishment reigned among the forces, so lately enterprising and resistless. Joan now called on the garrison no longer to stand upon the defensive, but boldly to attack the army of the besiegers. She took one redoubt and then another. The English, overwhelmed with amazement, scarcely dared to lift a hand against her. Their veteran generals became spellbound and powerless; and their soldiers were driven before the prophetess like a flock of sheep. The siege was raised.

Joan followed the English garrison to a fortified town which they fixed on as their place of retreat. The siege lasted ten days; the place was taken; and all the English within it made prisoners. The late victo-

rious forces now concentered themselves at Patay in
the Orleanois; Joan advanced to meet them. The battle lasted not a moment; it was rather a flight than a
combat; Fastolfe, one of the bravest of our commanders, threw down his arms, and ran for his life; Talbot
and Scales, the other generals, were made prisoners.
The siege of Orleans was raised on the eighth of May,
1429; the battle of Patay was fought on the tenth of
the following month. Joan was at this time twenty-
two years of age.

This extraordinary turn having been given to the
affairs of the kingdom, Joan next insisted that the
king should march to Rheims, in order to his being
crowned. Rheims lay in a direction expressly through
the midst of the enemies' garrisons. But every thing
yielded to the marvellous fortune that attended upon
the heroine. Troyes opened its gates; Chalons followed the example; Rheims sent a deputation with the
keys of the city, which met Charles on his march.
The proposed solemnity took place amidst the ecsta-
cies and enthusiastic shouts of his people. It was no
sooner over, than Joan stept forward. She said, she had
now performed the whole of what God had commissioned her to do; she was satisfied; she intreated the
king to dismiss her to the obscurity from which she
had sprung.

The ministers and generals of France however
found Joan too useful an instrument, to be willing
to part with her thus early; and she yielded to their
earnest expostulations. Under her guidance they

assailed Laon, Soissons, Chateau Thierry, Provins, and many other places, and took them one after another. She threw herself into Compiegne, which was besieged by the Duke of Burgundy in conjunction with certain English commanders. The day after her arrival she headed a sally against the enemy; twice she repelled them; but, finding their numbers increase every moment with fresh reinforcements, she directed a retreat. Twice she returned upon her pursuers, and made them recoil, the third time she was less fortunate. She found herself alone, surrounded with the enemy; and after having enacted prodigies of valour, she was compelled to surrender a prisoner. This happened on the twenty-fifth of May, 1430.

It remained to be determined what should be the fate of this admirable woman. Both friends and enemies agreed that her career had been attended with a supernatural power. The French, who were so infinitely indebted to her achievements, and who owed the sudden and glorious reverse of their affairs to her alone, were convinced that she was immediately commissioned by God, and vied with each other in reciting the miraculous phenomena which marked every step in her progress. The English, who saw all the victorious acquisitions of Henry V crumbling from their grasp, were equally impressed with the manifest miracle, but imputed all her good-fortune to a league with the prince of darkness. They said that her boasted visions were so many delusions of the devil. They determined to bring her to trial for the tremendous crimes of sorcery and witchcraft. They believed that, if she were once convicted and led out to execution, the prowess and valour which had hitherto marked their progress would return to them, and that they should obtain the same superiority over their disheartened foes. The devil, who had hitherto been her constant ally, terrified at the spectacle of the flames that consumed her, would instantly return to the infernal regions, and leave the field open to English enterprise and energy, and to the interposition of God and his saints.

An accusation was prepared against her, and all the solemnities of a public trial were observed. But the proofs were so weak and unsatisfactory, and Joan, though oppressed and treated with the utmost severity, displayed so much acuteness and presence of mind, that the court, not venturing to proceed to the last extremity, contented themselves with sentencing her to perpetual imprisonment, and to be allowed no other nourishment than bread and water for life. Before they yielded to this mitigation of punishment, they caused her to sign with her mark a recantation of her offences. She acknowledged that the enthusiasm that had guided her was an illusion, and promised never more to listen to its suggestions.

The hatred of her enemies however was not yet appeased. They determined in some way to entrap her. They had clothed her in a female garb; they insidiously laid in her way the habiliments of a man. The fire smothered in the bosom of the maid, revived at the sight; she was alone; she caught up the garments, and one by one adjusted them to her person. Spies were set upon her to watch for this event; they burst into the apartment. What she had done was construed into no less offence than that of a relapsed heretic; there was no more pardon for such confirmed delinquency; she was brought out to be burned alive in the market-place of Rouen, and she died, embracing a crucifix, and in her last moments calling upon the name of Jesus. A few days more than twelve months, had elapsed between the period of her first captivity and her execution...

Sanguinary Proceedings against Witchcraft.

I am now led to the most painful part of my subject, but which does not the less constitute one of its integral members, and which, though painful, is deeply instructive, and constitutes a most essential branch in the science of human nature. Wherever I could, I have endeavoured to render the topics which offered themselves to my examination, entertaining. When men pretended to invert the known laws of nature, "murdering impossibility; to make what cannot be, slight work;" I have been willing to consider the whole as an ingenious fiction, and merely serving as an example how far credulity could go in setting aside the deductions of our reason, and the evidence of sense. The artists in these cases did not fail to excite admiration, and gain some sort of applause from their contemporaries, though still with a tingling feeling that all was not exactly as it should be, and with a confession that the professors were exercising unhallowed arts. It was like what has been known of the art of acting; those who employed it were caressed and made every where welcome, but were not allowed the distinction of Christian burial.

But, particularly in the fifteenth century, things took a new turn. In the dawn of the day of good sense, and when historical evidence at length began to be weighed in the scales of judgment, men became less careless of truth, and regarded prodigies and miracles with a different temper. And, as it often happens, the crisis, the precise passage from ill to better, shewed itself more calamitous, and more full of enormities and atrocity, than the period when the understanding was completely hood-winked, and men digested absurdi-ties and impossibility with as much ease as their every day food. They would not now forgive the tampering with the axioms of eternal truth; they regarded cheat and imposture with a very different eye; and they had recourse to the stake and the faggot, for the purpose of proving that they would no longer be trifled with. They treated the offenders as the most atrocious of criminals, and thus, though by a very indirect and cir-cuitous method, led the way to the total dispersion of those clouds, which hung, with most uneasy opera-tion, on the human understanding.

The university of Paris in the year 1398 promul-gated an edict, in which they complained that the practice of witchcraft was become more frequent and general than at any former period.

A stratagem was at this time framed by the ecclesiastical persecutors, of confounding together the crimes of heresy and witchcraft. The first of these might seem to be enough in the days of bigotry and implicit faith, to excite the horror of the vulgar; but the advocates of religious uniformity held that they should be still more secure of their object, if they could combine the sin of holding cheap the authority of the recognised heads of Christian faith, with that of men's enlisting under the banners of Satan, and becoming the avowed and sworn vassals of his infernal empire. They accordingly seem to have invented the ideas of a sabbath of witches, a numerous assembly of persons who had cast off all sense of shame, and all regard for those things which the rest of the human species held most sacred, where the devil appeared among them in his most forbidding form, and, by rites equally ridiculous and obscene, the persons present acknowledged themselves his subjects. And, having invented this scene, these cunning and mischievous persecutors found means, as we shall presently see, of compelling their unfortunate victims to confess that they had personally assisted at the ceremony, and performed all the degrading offices which should consign them in the world to come to everlasting fire.

While I express myself thus, I by no means intend to encourage the idea that the ecclesiastical authorities of these times were generally hypocrites. They fully partook of the narrowness of thought of the period in which they lived. They believed that the sin of heretical pravity was "as the sin of witchcraft;" they regarded them alike with horror, and were persuaded that there was a natural consent and alliance between them. Fully impressed with this conception, they employed means from which our genuine and undebauched nature revolts, to extort from their deluded victims a confession of what their examiners apprehended to be true; they asked them leading questions; they suggested the answers they desired to receive; and led the ignorant and friendless to imagine that, if these answers were adopted, they might expect immediately to be relieved from insupportable tortures. The delusion went round. These unhappy wretches, finding themselves the objects of universal abhorrence, and the hatred of mankind, at length many of them believed that they had entered into a league with the devil, that they had been transported by him through the air to an assembly of souls consigned to everlasting reprobation, that they had bound themselves in acts of fealty to their infernal taskmasters, and had received from him in return the gift of performing superhuman and supernatural feats. This is a tremendous state of degradation of what Milton called the "the faultless proprieties of nature," which cooler thinking and more enlightened times would lead us to regard as impossible, but to which the uncontradicted and authentic voice of history compels us to subscribe.

The Albigenses and Waldenses were a set of men,

who, in the flourishing provinces of Languedoc, in the darkest ages, and when the understandings of human creatures by a force not less memorable than that of Procrustes were reduced to an uniform stature, shook off by some strange and unaccountable freak, the chains that were universally imposed, and arrived at a boldness of thinking similar to that which Luther and Calvin after a lapse of centuries advocated with happier auspices. With these manly and generous sentiments however they combined a considerable portion of wild enthusiasm. They preached the necessity of a community of goods, taught that it was necessary to wear sandals, because sandals only had been worn by the apostles, and devoted themselves to lives of rigorous abstinence and the most severe self-denial.

The Catholic church knew no other way in those days of converting heretics, but by fire and sword; and accordingly Pope Innocent the Third published a crusade against them. The inquisition was expressly appointed in its origin to bring back these stray sheep into the flock of Christ; and, to support this institution in its operations, Simon Montfort marched a numerous army for the extermination of the offenders. One hundred thousand are said to have perished. They disappeared from the country which had witnessed their commencement, and dispersed themselves in the vallies of Piedmont, in Artois, and in various other places. This crusade occurred in the commencement of the thirteenth century; and they do not again attract the notice of history till the middle of the fifteenth.

Monstrelet, in his Chronicle, gives one of the earliest accounts of the proceedings at this time instituted against these unfortunate people, under the date of the year 1459. "In this year," says he, "in the town of Arras, there occurred a miserable and inhuman scene, to which, I know not why, was given the name of Vaudoisie. There were taken up and imprisoned a number of considerable persons inhabitants of this town, and others of a very inferior class. These latter were so cruelly put to the torture, that they confessed, that they had been transported by supernatural means to a solitary place among woods, where the devil appeared before them in the form of a man, though they saw not his face. He instructed them in the way in which they should do his bidding, and exacted from them acts of homage and obedience. He feasted them, and after, having put out the lights, they proceeded to acts of the grossest licentiousness." These accounts, according to Monstrelet, were dictated to the victims by their tormentors; and they then added, under the same suggestion, the names of divers lords, prelates, and governors of towns and bailliages, whom they affirmed they had seen at these meetings, and who joined in the same unholy ceremonies. The historian adds, that it cannot be concealed that these accusations were brought by certain malicious persons, either to gratify an ancient hatred, or to extort from the rich sums of money, by means of which they might purchase their escape from further prosecution. The persons apprehended were many of them put to the torture so severely, and for so long a time, and were tortured again and again, that they were obliged to confess what was laid to their charge. Some however shewed so great constancy, that they could by no means be induced to depart from the protestation of their innocence. In fine, many of the poorer victims were inhumanly burned; while the richer with great sums of money procured their discharge, but at the same time were compelled to banish themselves to distant places, remote from the scene of this cruel outrage.—Balduinus of Artois gives a similar account, and adds that the sentence of the judges was brought, by appeal under the revision of the parliament of Paris, and was reversed by that judicature in the year 1491.

I have not succeeded in tracing to my satisfaction from the original authorities the dates of the following examples, and therefore shall refer them to the periods assigned them in Hutchinson on Witchcraft. The facts themselves rest for the most part on the most unquestionable authority.

Innocent VIII published about the year 1484 a bull, in which he affirms: "It has come to our ears, that numbers of both sexes do not avoid to have intercourse with the infernal fiends, and that by their sorceries they afflict both man and beast; they blight the marriage-bed, destroy the births of women, and the increase of cattle; they blast the corn on the ground, the grapes of the vineyard, the fruits of the trees, and the grass and herbs of the field." For these reasons he arms the inquisitors with apostolic power to "imprison, convict and punish" all such as may be charged with these offences.—The consequences of this edict were dreadful all over the continent, particularly in Italy, Germany and France.

Alciatus, an eminent lawyer of this period, relates, that a certain inquisitor came about this time into the vallies of the Alps, being commissioned to enquire out and proceed against heretical women with whom those parts were infested. He accordingly consigned more than one hundred to the flames, every day, like a new holocaust, sacrificing such persons to Vulcan, as, in the judgment of the historian, were subjects demanding rather hellebore than fire; till at length the peasantry of the vicinity rose in arms, and drove the merciless judge out of the country. The culprits were accused of having dishonoured the crucifix, and denying Christ for their God. They were asserted to have solemnised after a detestable way the devil's sabbath, in which the fiend appeared personally among them, and instructed them in the ceremonies of his worship. Meanwhile a question was raised whether they personally assisted on the occasion, or only saw the solemnities in a vision, credible witnesses having sworn that they were at home in their beds, at the very time that they were accused of having taken part in these blasphemies.

In 1515, more than five hundred persons are said to have suffered capitally for the crime of witchcraft in the city of Geneva in the course of three months.

In 1524, one thousand persons were burned on this

accusation in the territory of Como, and one hundred per annum for several year after.

Danaeus commences his Dialogue of Witches with this observation. "Within three months of the present time (1575) an almost infinite number of witches have been taken, on whom the parliament of Paris has passed judgment: and the same tribunal fails not to sit daily, as malefactors accused of this crime are continually brought before them out of all the provinces."

In the year 1595 Nicholas Remi, otherwise Remigius, printed a very curious work, entitled Demonolatreia, in which he elaborately expounds the principles of the compact into which the devil enters with his mortal allies, and the modes of conduct specially observed by both parties. He boasts that his exposition is founded on an exact observation of the judicial proceedings which had taken place under his eye in the duchy of Lorraine, where for the preceding fifteen years nine hundred persons, more or less, had suffered the extreme penalty of the law for the crime of sorcery. Most of the persons tried seem to have been sufficiently communicative as to the different kinds of menace and compulsion by which the devil had brought them into his terms, and the various appearances he had exhibited, and feats he had performed: but others, says the author, had, "by preserving an obstinate silence, shewn themselves invincible to every species of torture that could be inflicted on them."

But the most memorable record that remains to us

146

on the subject of witchcraft, is contained in an ample quarto volume, entitled A Representation (Tableau) of the Ill Faith of Evil Spirits and Demons, by Pierre De Lancre, Royal Counsellor in the Parliament of Bordeaux. This man was appointed with one coadjutor, to enquire into certain acts of sorcery, reported to have been committed in the district of Labourt, near the foot of the Pyrenees; and his commission bears date in May, 1609, and by consequence twelve months before the death of Henry the Fourth.

The book is dedicated to M. de Silleri, chancellor of France; and in the dedication the author observes, that formerly those who practised sorcery were well known for persons of obscure station and narrow intellect; but that now the sorcerers who confess their misdemeanours, depose, that there are seen in the customary meetings held by such persons a great number of individuals of quality, whom Satan keeps veiled from ordinary gaze, and who are allowed to approach near to him, while those of a poorer and more vulgar class are thrust back to the furthest part of the assembly. The whole narrative assumes the form of a regular warfare between Satan on the one side, and the royal commissioners on the other.

At first the devil endeavoured to supply the accused with strength to support the tortures by which it was sought to extort confession from them, insomuch that, in an intermission of the torture, the wretches declared that, presently falling asleep, they seemed to be in paradise, and to enjoy the most beautiful

147

visions. The commissioners however, observing this, took care to grant them scarcely any remission, till they had drawn from them, if possible, an ample confession. The devil next proceeded to stop the mouths of the accused that they might not confess. He leaped on their throats, and evidently caused an obstruction of the organs of speech, so that in vain they endeavoured to relieve themselves by disclosing all that was demanded of them.

The historian proceeds to say that, at these sacrilegious assemblings, they now began to murmur against the devil, as wanting power to relieve them in their extremity. The children, the daughters, and other relatives of the victims reproached him, not scrupling to say, "Out upon you! you promised that our mothers who were prisoners should not die; and look how you have kept your word with us! They have been burned, and are a heap of ashes." In answer to this charge the devil stoutly affirmed, that their parents, who seemed to have suffered, were not dead, but were safe in a foreign country, assuring the malcontents that, if they called on them, they would receive an answer. The children called accordingly, and by an infernal illusion an answer came, exactly in the several voices of the deceased, declaring that they were in a state of happiness and security.

Further to satisfy the complainers, the devil produced illusory fires, and encouraged the dissatisfied to walk through them, assuring them that the fires lighted by a judicial decree were as harmless and inoffensive as these. The demon further threatened that he would cause the prosecutors to be burned in their own fire, and even proceeded to make them in semblance hover and alight on the branches of the neighbouring trees. He further caused a swarm of toads to appear like a garland to crown the heads of the sufferers, at which when in one instance the bystanders threw stones to drive them away, one monstrous black toad remained to the last uninjured, and finally mounted aloft, and vanished from sight. De Lancre goes on to describe the ceremonies of the sabbath of the devil; and a plate is inserted, presenting the assembly in the midst of their solemnities. He describes in several chapters the sort of contract entered into between the devil and the sorcerers, the marks by which they may be known, the feast with which the demon regaled them, their distorted and monstrous dance, the cop-ulation between the fiend and the witch, and its issue.—It is easy to imagine with what sort of fairness the trials were conducted, when such is the descrip-tion the judge affords us of what passed at these assem-blies. Six hundred were burned under this prosecu-tion...

10

The Life and Times of Dr. Faust

The historical figure Dr. Johann Georg Faust lived during the late fifteenth and early sixteenth centuries, traveling the German-speaking states as one peripatetic magician among many. He was indeed a real person, though readers are most likely familiar with the name from Goethe's famous plays. The historical Faust was educated at Heidelberg and scattered records indicate that he may have moved from place to place, peddling various magic acts, alchemists' schemes, and a variety of criminal behavior. Faust worked as an astrologer and necromancer across a number of German cities before his violent—perhaps chemically explosive—death (see below). Though Faust's historical life is extremely poorly documented, his legend is lush and vibrant field for scholarly inquiry. His life and personage were well known by contemporary standards of living, non-royal figures but within several decades after his death the new art of printing made Faust famous throughout Europe. In courts and gutters alike, one could read cheap books which regaled and terrified the audience with tales of the demon-conjuring, necromantic Dr. Faust.

In tales of his wild and untamed life, readers could no doubt see themselves, like Faust, confronted with the very real choice to give oneself entirely to evil or preserve whatever goodness remained in man after the Fall. We all possess power and therefore the ability to pursue our own desires at the expense of others'. Should we, like Faust, cast ourselves and all we are upon the altar of power, so that we may reap tremendous rewards for a time—even a very long time—but in doing so, incur the distrust, malefi-cence, and even rage of our mistreated fellows. Power may indeed be satisfying and productive, but *for whom?* Defrauding or dominating one's peers may yield great material and psychological rewards, but the costs included the erection of class barriers between the exploiter and the exploited. On the one side stood men like Faust, essen-tially running for his life from town to town to test the next scheme and live for a while on the fruits of the last. On the other stood his dupes, united in their opposition to someone who would resort to such unseemly and dia-bolical means to achieve power, wealth, long life, and influ-

151

ence. With such a combination of moral unscrupulousness and satanic strength supporting his will, how could his various neighbors ever trust Faust for long?

Such is the spirit in which William Godwin approaches the subject. Whether Faust even existed, Godwin believed the iconic legend communicates larger psychological and sociological points about devilry and witchcraft extremely well. Faust was so willing to enjoy the liberties, luxuries, and powers afforded him by the devil that he sacrificed his very soul. Though devil incantation and demonic privilege may be fictional phenomenon, the examples nonetheless provide us windows into the mind of those who would stop at *nothing* to achieve their will.

Sanguinary Proceedings against Witchcraft.

Faustus.

Next...comes the celebrated Dr. Faustus. Little in point of fact is known respecting this eminent personage in the annals of necromancy. His pretended history does not seem to have been written till about the year 1587, perhaps half a century after his death. This work is apparently in its principal features altogether fictitious. We have no reason however to deny the early statements as to his life. He is asserted by Camerarius and Wierus to have been born at Cundling near Cracow in the kingdom of Poland, and is understood to have passed the principal part of his life at the university of Wittenberg. He was probably well known to Cornelius Agrippa and Paracelsus. Melancthon mentions him in his Letters; and Conrad Gessner refers to him as a contemporary...He was probably nothing more than an accomplished juggler, who appears to have practised his art with great success in several towns of Germany. He was also no doubt a pretender to necromancy.

...Faustus then, according to his history, was the son of a peasant, residing on the banks of the Roda in the duchy of Weimar, and was early adopted by an uncle, dwelling in the city of Wittenberg, who had no children. Here he was sent to college, and was soon distinguished by the greatness of his talents, and the rapid progress he made in every species of learning that was put before him. He was destined by his relative to the profession of theology. But singularly enough, considering that he is represented as furnishing materials for his own Memoirs, he is said ungraciously to have set at nought his uncle's pious intentions by deriding God's word, and thus to have resembled Cain, Reuben and Absalom, who, having sprung from godly parents, afflicted their fathers' hearts by their apostasy. He went through his examinations with applause, and carried off all the first prizes among sixteen competitors. He therefore obtained the degree of doctor in divinity; but his success only made him the more proud and headstrong. He disdained his theological eminence, and sighed for distinction as a man of the world. He took his degree as a doctor of medicine, and aspired to celebrity as a practitioner of physic. About the same time he fell in with certain contemporaries, of tastes similar to his own, and associated with them in the study of Chaldean, Greek and Arabic science, of strange incantations and supernatural influences, in short, of all the arts of a sorcerer.

Having made such progress as he could by dint of study and intense application, he at length resolved to prosecute his purposes still further by actually raising the devil. He happened one evening to walk in a thick, dark wood, within a short distance from Wittenberg, when it occurred to him that that was a fit place for executing his design. He stopped at a solitary spot where four roads met, and made use of his wand to mark out a large circle, and then two small ones within the larger. In one of these he fixed himself, appropriating the other for the use of his expected visitor. He went over the precise range of charms and incantations, omitting nothing. It was now dark night between the ninth and tenth hour. The devil manifested himself by the usual signs of his appearance. "Wherefore am I called?" said he, "and what is it that you demand?" "I require," rejoined Faustus, "that you should sedulously attend upon me, answer my enquiries, and fulfil my behests."

Immediately upon Faustus pronouncing these words, there followed a tumult over head, as if heaven and earth were coming together. The trees in their topmost branches bended to their very roots. It seemed as if the whole forest were peopled with devils, making a crash like a thousand waggons, hurrying to the right and the left, before and behind, in every possible direction, with thunder and lightning, and the continual discharge of great cannon. Hell appeared to have emptied itself, to have furnished the din. There succeeded the most charming music from all sorts of instruments, and sounds of hilarity and dancing. Next came a report as of a tournament, and the clashing of innumerable lances. This lasted so long, that Faustus was many times about to rush out of the circle in which he had inclosed himself, and to abandon his preparations. His courage and resolution however got the better; and he remained immoveable. He pursued his incantations without intermission. Then came to the very edge of the circle a griffin first, and next a dragon, which in the midst of his enchantments grinned at him horribly with his teeth, but finally fell down at his feet, and extended his length to many a rood. Faustus persisted. Then succeeded a sort of fireworks, a pillar of fire, and a man on fire at the top, who leaped down; and there immediately appeared a number of globes here and there red-hot, while the man on fire went and came to every part of the circle for a quarter of an hour. At length the devil came forward in the shape of a grey monk, and asked Faustus what he wanted. Faustus adjourned their further conference, and appointed the devil to come to him at his lodgings.

He in the mean time busied himself in the necessary preparations. He entered his study at the appointed time, and found the devil waiting for him. Faustus told him that he had prepared certain articles, to which it was necessary that the demon should fully accord,—that he should attend him at all times, when required, for all the days of his life, that he should bring him every thing he wanted, that he should come to him in any shape that Faustus required, or be invisible, and Faustus should be invisible too, whenever he desired it, that he should deny him nothing, and answer him with perfect veracity to every thing he demanded. To some of these requisitions the spirit could not consent, without authority from his master, the chief of devils. At length all these concessions were adjusted. The devil on his part also prescribed his conditions. That Faustus should abjure the Christian religion and all reverence for the supreme God; that he should enjoy the entire command of his attendant demon for a certain term of years, and that at the end of that period the devil should dispose of him body and soul at his pleasure [the term was fixed for twenty-four years]; that he should at all times stedfastly refuse to listen to any one who should desire to convert him, or convince him of the error of his ways, and lead him to repentance; that Faustus should draw up a writing containing these particulars, and sign it with his blood, that he should deliver this writing to the devil, and keep a duplicate of it for himself, that so there might be no misunderstanding. It was further appointed by Faustus that the devil should usually attend him in the habit of cordelier, with a pleasing countenance and an insinuating demeanour. Faustus also asked the devil his name, who answered that he was usually called Mephostophiles (perhaps more accurately Nephostophiles, a lover of clouds).

Previously to this deplorable transaction, in which Faustus sold himself, soul and body, to the devil, he had consumed his inheritance, and was reduced to great poverty. But he was now no longer subjected to any straits. The establishments of the prince of Chutz, the duke of Bavaria, and the archbishop of Saltzburgh were daily put under contribution for his more convenient supply. By the diligence of Mephostophiles provisions of all kinds continually flew in at his windows; and the choicest wines were perpetually found at his board to the annoyance and discredit of the cellarers and butlers of these eminent personages, who were extremely blamed for defalcations in which they had no share. He also brought him a monthly supply of money, sufficient for the support of his establishment. Besides, he supplied him with a succession of mistresses, such as his heart desired, which were in truth nothing but devils disguised under the semblance of beautiful women. He further gave to Faustus a book, in which were amply detailed the processes of sorcery and witchcraft, by means of which the doctor could obtain whatever he desired.

One of the earliest indulgences which Faustus proposed to himself from the command he possessed over his servant-demon, was the gratification of his curiosity in surveying the various nations of the world. Accordingly Mephostophiles converted himself into a horse, with two hunches on his back like a dromedary, between which he conveyed Faustus through the air where-ever he desired. They consumed fifteen months in their travels. Among the countries they visited the history mentions Pannonia, Austria, Germany, Bohemia, Silesia, Saxony, Misnia, Thuringia, Franconia, Suabia, Bavaria, Lithuania, Livonia, Prussia, Muscovy, Friseland, Holland, Westphalia, Zealand, Brabant, Flanders, France, Spain, Italy, Poland, and Hungary; and afterwards Turkey, Egypt, England, Sweden, Denmark, India, Africa and Persia. In most of these countries Mephostophiles points out to his fellow-traveller their principal curiosities and antiquities. In Rome they sojourned three days and three nights, and, being themselves invisible, visited the residence of the pope and the other principal palaces.

At Constantinople Faustus visited the emperor of the Turks, assuming to himself the figure of the prophet Mahomet. His approach was preceded by a splendid illumination, not less than that of the sun in all his glory. He said to the emperor, "Happy art thou, oh sultan, who art found worthy to be visited by the great prophet." And the emperor in return fell prostrate before him, thanking Mahomet for his condescension in this visit. The doctor also entered the seraglio, where he remained six days under the same figure, the building and its gardens being all the time environed with a thick darkness, so that no one, not the emperor himself, dared to enter. At the end of this time the doctor, still under the figure of Mahomet, was publicly seen, ascending, as it seemed, to heaven. The sultan afterwards enquired of the women of his seraglio what had occurred to them during the period of the darkness; and they answered, that the God Mahomet had been with them, that he had enjoyed them corporeally, and had told them that from his seed should arise a great people, capable of irresistible exploits.

Faustus had conceived a plan of making his way into the terrestrial paradise, without awakening suspicion in his demon-conductor. For this purpose he ordered him to ascend the highest mountains of Asia. At length they came so near, that they saw the angel with the flaming sword forbidding approach to the garden. Faustus, perceiving this, asked Mephostophiles what it meant. His conductor told him, but added that it was in vain for them, or any one but the angels of the Lord, to think of entering within.

Having gratified his curiosity in other ways, Faustus was seized with a vehement desire to visit the infernal regions. He proposed the question to Mephostophiles, who told him that this was a matter out of his department, and that on that journey he could have no other conductor than Beelzebub. Accordingly, every thing being previously arranged, one day at midnight Beelzebub appeared, being already equipped with a saddle made of dead men's bones. Faustus speedily mounted. They in a short time came to an abyss, and encountered a multitude of enormous serpents; but a bear with wings came to their aid, and drove the serpents away. A flying bull next came with a hideous roar, so fierce that Beelzebub appeared to give way, and Faustus tumbled at once heels-over-head into the pit. After having fallen to a considerable depth, two dragons with a chariot came to his aid, and an ape helped him to get into the vehicle. Presently however came on a storm with thunder and lightning, so dreadful that the doctor was thrown out, and sunk in a tempestuous sea to a vast depth. He contrived however to lay hold of a rock, and here to secure himself a footing. He looked down, and perceived a great gulph, in which lay floating many of the vulgar, and not a few emperors, kings, princes, and such as had been mighty lords. Faustus with a sudden impulse cast himself into the midst of the flames with which they were surrounded, with the desire to snatch one of the damned souls from the pit. But, just as he thought he had caught him by the hand, the miserable wretch slided from between his fingers, and sank again.

At length the doctor became wholly exhausted with the fatigue he had undergone, with the smoke and the fog, with the stifling, sulphureous air, with the tempestuous blasts, with the alternate extremes of heat and cold, and with the clamours, the lamentations, the agonies, and the howlings of the damned every-where around him,—when, just in the nick of time, Beelzebub appeared to him again, and invited him once more to ascend the saddle, which he had occupied during his infernal journey. Here he fell asleep, and, when he awoke, found himself in his own bed in his house. He then set himself seriously to reflect on what had passed. At one time he believed that he had been really in hell, and had witnessed all its secrets. At another he became persuaded that he had been subject to an illusion only, and that the devil had led him through an imaginary scene, which was truly the case; for the devil had taken care not to shew him the real hell, fearing that it might have caused too great a terror, and have induced him to repent him of his misdeeds perhaps before it was too late...

In another instance, Faustus went into a fair, mounted on a noble beast, richly caparisoned, the sight of which presently brought all the horse-fanciers about him. After considerable haggling, he at last disposed of his horse to a dealer for a handsome price, only cautioning him at parting, how he rode the horse to water. The dealer, despising the caution that had been given him, turned his horse the first thing towards the river. He had however no sooner plunged in, than the horse vanished, and the rider found himself seated on a saddle of straw, in the middle of the stream. With difficulty he waded to the shore, and immediately, enquiring out the doctor's inn, went to him to complain of the cheat. He was directed to

Faustus's room, and entering found the conjuror on his bed, apparently asleep. He called to him lustily, but the doctor took no notice. Worked up beyond his patience, he next laid hold of Faustus's foot, that he might rouse him the more effectually. What was his surprise, to find the doctor's leg and foot come off in his hand! Faustus screamed, apparently in agony of pain, and the dealer ran out of the room as fast as he could, thinking that he had the devil behind him...

When the doctor happened to be at Frankfort, there came there four conjurors, who obtained vast applause by the trick of cutting off one another's heads, and fastening them on again. Faustus was exasperated at this proceeding, and regarded them as laying claim to a skill superior to his own. He went, and was invisibly present at their exhibition. They placed beside them a vessel with liquor which they pretended was the elixir of life, into which at each time they threw a plant resembling the lily, which no sooner touched the liquor than its buds began to unfold, and shortly it appeared in full blossom. The chief conjuror watched his opportunity; and, when the charm was complete, made no more ado but struck off the head of his fellow that was next to him, and dipping it in the liquor, adjusted it to the shoulders, where it became as securely fixed as before the operation. This was repeated a second and a third time. At length it came to the turn of the chief conjuror to have his head smitten off. Faustus stood by invisibly, and at the proper time broke off the flower of the lily without any one being aware of it. The head therefore of the principal conjuror was struck off; but in vain was it steeped in the liquor. The other conjurors were at a loss to account for the disappearance of the lily, and fumbled for a long time with the old sorcerer's head, which would not stick on in any position in which it could be placed...

One Christmas-time Faustus gave a grand entertainment to certain distinguished persons of both sexes at Wittenberg. To render the scene more splendid, he contrived to exhibit a memorable inversion of the seasons. As the company approached the doctor's house, they were surprised to find, though there was a heavy snow through the neighbouring fields, that Faustus's court and garden bore not the least marks of the season, but on the contrary were green and blooming as in the height of summer. There was an appearance of the freshest vegetation, together with a beautiful vineyard, abounding with grapes, figs, raspberries, and an exuberance of the finest fruits. The large, red Provence roses, were as sweet to the scent as the eye, and looked perfectly fresh and sparkling with dew.

As Faustus was now approaching the last year of his term, he seemed to resolve to pamper his appetite with every species of luxury. He carefully accumulated all the materials of voluptuousness and magnificence. He was particularly anxious in the selection of women who should serve for his pleasures. He had one Englishwoman, one Hungarian, one French, two of Germany, and two from different parts of Italy, all of them eminent for the perfections which characterised their different countries.

As Faustus's demeanour was particularly engaging, there were many respectable persons in the city in which he lived, that became interested in his welfare. These applied to a certain monk of exemplary purity of life and devotion, and urged him to do every thing he could to rescue the doctor from impending destruction. The monk began with him with tender and pathetic remonstrances. He then drew a fearful picture of the wrath of God, and the eternal damnation which would certainly ensue. He reminded the doctor of his extraordinary gifts and graces, and told him how different an issue might reasonably have been expected from him. Faustus listened attentively to all the good monk said, but replied mournfully that it was too late, that he had despised and insulted the Lord, that he had deliberately sealed a solemn compact to the devil, and that there was no possibility of going back. The monk answered, "You are mistaken. Cry to the Lord for grace; and it shall still be given. Shew true remorse; confess your sins; abstain for the future from all acts of sorcery and diabolical interference; and you may rely on final salvation." The doctor however felt that all endeavours would be hopeless, He found in himself an incapacity, for true repentance. And finally the devil came to him, reproached him for breach of contract in listening to the pious expostulations of a saint, threatened that in case of infidelity he would take him away to hell even before his time, and frightened the doctor into the act of signing a fresh contract in ratification of that which he had signed before.

At length Faustus ultimately arrived at the end of the term for which he had contracted with the devil. For two or three years before it expired, his character gradually altered. He became subject to fits of despondency, was no longer susceptible of mirth and amusement, and reflected with bitter agony on the close in which the whole must terminate. During the last month of his period, he no longer sought the services of his infernal ally, but with the utmost unwillingness saw his arrival. But Mephostophiles now attended him unbidden, and treated him with biting scoffs and reproaches. "You have well studied the Scriptures," he said, "and ought to have known that your safety lay in worshipping God alone. You sinned with your eyes open, and can by no means plead ignorance. You thought that twenty-four years was a term that would have no end; and you now see how rapidly it is flitting away. The term for which you sold yourself to the devil is a very different thing; and, after the lapse of thousands of ages, the prospect before you will be still as unbounded as ever. You were warned; you were earnestly pressed to repent; but now it is too late."

After the demon, Mephostophiles, had long tormented Faustus in this manner, he suddenly disappeared, consigning him over to wretchedness, vexation and despair.

The whole twenty-four years were now expired. The day before, Mephostophiles again made his appearance, holding in his hand the bond which the doctor had signed with his blood, giving him notice that the next day, the devil, his master, would come for him, and advising him to hold himself in readiness. Faustus, it seems, had earned himself much good will among the younger members of the university by his agreeable manners, by his willingness to oblige them, and by the extraordinary spectacles with which he occasionally diverted them. This day he resolved to pass in a friendly farewel. He invited a number of them to meet him at a house of public reception, in a hamlet adjoining to the city. He bespoke a large room in the house for a banqueting room, another apartment overhead for his guests to sleep in, and a smaller chamber at a little distance for himself. He furnished his table with abundance of delicacies and wines. He endeavoured to appear among them in high spirits; but his heart was inwardly sad.

When the entertainment was over, Faustus addressed them, telling them that this was the last day of his life, reminding them of the wonders with which he had frequently astonished them, and informing them of the condition upon which he had held this power. They, one and all, expressed the deepest sorrow at the intelligence. They had had the idea of something unlawful in his proceedings; but their notions had been very far from coming up to the truth. They regretted exceedingly that he had not been unreserved in his communications at an earlier period. They would have had recourse in his behalf to the means of religion, and have applied to pious men, desiring them to employ their power to intercede with heaven in his favour. Prayer and penitence might have done much for him; and the mercy of heaven was unbounded. They advised him still to call upon God, and endeavour to secure an interest in the merits of the Saviour.

Faustus assured them that it was all in vain, and that his tragical fate was inevitable. He led them to their sleeping apartment, and recommended to them to pass the night as they could, but by no means, whatever they might happen to hear, to come out of it; as their interference could in no way be beneficial to him, and might be attended with the most serious injury to themselves. They lay still therefore, as he had enjoined them; but not one of them could close his eyes.

Between twelve and one in the night they heard first a furious storm of wind round all sides of the house, as if it would have torn away the walls from their foundations. This no sooner somewhat abated, than a noise was heard of discordant and violent hissing, as if the house was full of all sorts of venomous reptiles, but which plainly proceeded from Faustus's chamber. Next they heard the doctor's room-door vehemently burst open, and cries for help uttered with dreadful agony, but a half-suppressed voice, which presently grew fainter and fainter. Then every thing became still, as if the everlasting motion of the world was suspended.

When at length it became broad day, the students

went in a body into the doctor's apartment. But he was no where to be seen. Only the walls were found smeared with his blood, and marks as if his brains had been dashed out. His body was finally discovered at some distance from the house, his limbs dismembered, and marks of great violence about the features of his face. The students gathered up the mutilated parts of his body, and afforded them private burial at the temple of Mars in the village where he died.

[Some scholars] have carried their scepticism so far, as to have started a doubt whether there was ever really such a person as Faustus of Wittenberg, the alleged magician. But the testimony of Wierus, Philip Camerarius, Melancthon and others, his contemporaries, sufficiently refutes this supposition. The fact is, that there was undoubtedly such a man, who, by sleights of dexterity, made himself a reputation as if there was something supernatural in his performances, and that he was probably also regarded with a degree of terror and abhorrence by the superstitious. On this theme was constructed a romance, which once possessed the highest popularity, and furnished a subject to the dramatical genius of Marlow, Leasing, Goethe, and others.—It is sufficiently remarkable, that the notoriety of this romance seems to have suggested to Shakespear the idea of sending the grand conception of his brain, Hamlet, prince of Denmark, to finish his education at the university of Wittenberg.

And here it may not be uninstructive to remark the different tone of the record of the acts of Ziito, the

Bohemian, and Faustus of Wittenburg, though little more than half a century elapsed between the periods at which they were written. Dubravius, bishop of Olmutz in Moravia, to whose pen we are indebted for what we know of Ziito, died in the year 1553. He has deemed it not unbecoming to record in his national history of Bohemia, the achievements of this magician, who, he says, exhibited them before Wenceslaus, king of the country, at the celebration of his marriage. A waggon-load of sorcerers arrived at Prague on that occasion for the entertainment of the company. But, at the close of that century, the exploits of Faustus were no longer deemed entitled to a place in national history, but were more appropriately taken for the theme of a romance. Faustus and his performances were certainly contemplated with at least as much horror as the deeds of Ziito. But popular credulity was no longer wound to so high a pitch: the marvels effected by Faustus are not represented as challenging the observation of thousands at a public court, and on the occasion of a royal festival. They "hid their diminished heads," and were performed comparatively in a corner...

11

Quacks & Hucksters

In the next set of entries, our author continues to shift his main theme from earlier examples of occultists dominating the affairs of men through exploitative trickery to the transformation of witches into a persecuted class of troubled individuals. Joan of Arc was executed for fear of her communications with demons and witch trials proliferated throughout Europe during the late medieval period, but Godwin takes great care to steadily remind us that these people were *not actually necromancers.* They were mere quacks—cold-blooded quacks with ill-will in many cases but mere quacks nonetheless. Many of them, like Joan and our earlier papal sorcerers, were genuine enthusiasts who truly believed in mystical power. Others simply sought to get a piece of the church and state's action by exploiting public ignorance for personal gain.

As two case studies in the latter form of *mere huckster-ism*, Godwin offers Benvenuto Cellini's story of a priest and his "magic lantern" followed by a short biography of John Dee. Cellini's Sicilian priest seems to have filled the same niche that modern New Orleans tourist Voodoo shops occupy—he essentially offered an elaborate and ceremonial show which seemed sufficiently authentic and complex to convince Cellini that the causes were mystical rather than technological. John Dee was a mathematician and Queen Elizabeth I's court astrologer before he was a degenerating traveling salesman of useless philosopher's stones. His rise to the heights of power and influence and consequent decline to the depths of failure and despair is in many ways emblematic of the Faustian bargain's usual outcome: those who grasp endlessly after power place themselves in the positions most vulnerable to the avarice of other powerful people. In John Dee's case, his entire career was built on astrological and alchemical promises which he constantly failed to deliver, leaving him entirely at the mercy of those still more powerful than he. By plac-ing their entire ethics, their senses of personal identity, and the bulk of their natural lives under the command of power's dictates, they condemned themselves to be the victims of power's demands. Joan of Arc and John Dee may both have been quacks, but who can deny that there is greater dignity and respect in Joan's genuine enthusiasm than in John's *mere hucksterism*?

Sanguinary Proceedings against Witchcraft.

Quacks, Who in Cool Blood Undertook to Overreach Mankind.

Hitherto we have principally passed such persons in review, as seem to have been in part at least the victims of their own delusions. But beside these there has always been a numerous class of men, who, with minds perfectly disengaged and free, have applied themselves to concert the means of overreaching the simplicity, or baffling the penetration, of those who were merely spectators, and uninitiated in the mystery of the arts that were practised upon them. Such was no doubt the case with the speaking heads and statues, which were sometimes exhibited in the ancient oracles. Such was the case with certain optical delusions, which were practised on the unsuspecting, and were contrived to produce on them the effect of supernatural revelations. Such is the story of Bel and the Dragon in the book of Apocrypha, where the priests daily placed before the idol twelve measures of flour, and forty sheep, and six vessels of wine, pretending that the idol consumed all these provisions, when in fact they entered the temple by night, by a door under the altar, and removed them.

Benvenuto Cellini.

We have a story minutely related by Benvenuto Cellini in his Life, which it is now known was produced by optical delusion, but which was imposed upon the artist and his companions as altogether supernatural. It occurred a very short time before the death of pope Clement the Seventh in 1534, and is thus detailed. It took place in the Coliseum at Rome.

"It came to pass through a variety of odd accidents, that I made acquaintance with a Sicilian priest, who was a man of genius, and well versed in the Greek and Latin languages. Happening one day to have some conversation with him, where the subject turned upon the art of necromancy, I, who had a great desire to know something of the matter, told him, that I had all my life had a curiosity to be acquainted with the mysteries of this art. The priest made answer, that the man must be of a resolute and steady temper, who entered on that study. I replied, that I had fortitude and resolution enough to desire to be initiated in it. The priest subjoined, 'If you think you have the heart to venture, I will give you all the satisfaction you can desire.' Thus we agreed to enter upon a scheme of necromancy.

"The priest one evening prepared to satisfy me...We repaired to the Coliseum; and the priest, according to the custom of conjurors, began to draw circles on the ground, with the most impressive ceremonies imaginable. He likewise brought with him all sorts of precious perfumes and fire, with some compositions which diffused noisome and bad odours. As soon as he was in readiness, he made an opening to the circle, and took us by the hand, and ordered the other necromancer, his partner, to throw perfumes into the fire at a proper time, intrusting the care of the fire and the perfumes to the rest; and then he began his incantations.

"This ceremony lasted above an hour and a half, when there appeared several legions of devils, so that the amphitheatre was quite filled with them. I was busy about the perfumes, when the priest, who knew that there was a sufficient number of infernal spirits, turned about to me, and said, 'Benvenuto, ask them something.' I answered, 'Let them bring me into company with my Sicilian mistress, Angelica.' That night we obtained no answer of any sort; but I received great satisfaction in having my curiosity so far indulged.

"The necromancer told me that it was requisite we should go a second time, assuring me that I should be satisfied in whatever I asked; but that I must bring with me a boy that had never known woman. I took with me my apprentice, who was about twelve years of age...When we came to the place appointed, the priest, having made his preparations as before with the same and even more striking ceremonies, placed us within the circle, which he had drawn with a more wonderful art and in a more solemn manner, than at our former meeting. Thus having committed the care

of the perfumes and the fire to my friend Vincenzio,
who was assisted by Gaddi, he put into my hands a
pintacolo, or magical chart, and bid me turn it towards
the places to which he should direct me; and under
the *pintacolo* I held my apprentice. The necromancer,
having begun to make his most tremendous invoca-
tions, called by their names a multitude of demons
who were the leaders of the several legions, and questioned them, by the virtue and power of the eternal,
uncreated God, who lives for ever, in the Hebrew
language, as also in Latin and Greek; insomuch that
the amphitheatre was filled, almost in an instant, with
demons a hundred times more numerous than at the
former conjuration. Vincenzio meanwhile was busied
in making a fire with the assistance of Gaddi, and
burning a great quantity of precious perfumes. I, by
the direction of the necromancer, again desired to be
in company with my Angelica. He then turning upon
me said, 'Know, they have declared that in the space
of a month you shall be in her company.'

"He then requested me to stand by him resolutely,
because the legions were now above a thousand more
in number than he had designed; and besides these
were the most dangerous; so that, after they had
answered my question, it behoved him to be civil to
them, and dismiss them quietly. At the same time the
boy under the *pintacolo* was in a terrible fright, saying, that there were in the place a million of fierce
men who threatened to destroy us; and that, besides,
there were four armed giants of enormous stature,

175

who endeavoured to break into our circle. During this time, while the necromancer, trembling with fear, endeavoured by mild means to dismiss them in the best way he could, Vincenzio, who quivered like an aspen leaf, took care of the perfumes. Though I was as much afraid as any of them, I did my utmost to conceal it; so that I greatly contributed to inspire the rest with resolution; but the truth is, I gave myself over for a dead man, seeing the horrid fright the necromancer was in.

"The boy had placed his head between his knees; and said, 'In this attitude will I die; for we shall all surely perish.' I told him that those demons were under us, and what he saw was smoke and shadow; so bid him hold up his head and take courage. No sooner did he look up, than he cried out, 'The whole amphitheatre is burning, and the fire is just falling on us.' So, covering his eyes with his hands, he again exclaimed, that destruction was inevitable, and he desired to see no more. The necromancer intreated me to have a good heart, and to take care to burn proper perfumes; upon which I turned to Vincenzio, and bade him burn all the most precious perfumes he had. At the same time I cast my eyes upon Gaddi, who was terrified to such a degree, that he could scarcely distinguish objects, and seemed to be half dead. Seeing him in this condition, I said to him, 'Gaddi, upon these occasions a man should not yield to fear, but stir about to give some assistance; so come directly, and put on more of these perfumes.' Gaddi accordingly attempted to move; but the effect was annoying both to our sense of hearing and smell, and overcame the perfumes.

"The boy perceiving this, once more ventured to raise his head, and, seeing me laugh, began to take courage, and said, 'The devils are flying away with a vengeance.' In this condition we staid, till the bell rang for morning prayers. The boy again told us, that there remained but few devils, and those were at a great distance. When the magician had performed the rest of his ceremonies, he stripped off his gown, and took up a wallet full of books, which he had brought with him. We all went out of the circle together, keeping as close to each other as we possibly could, especially the boy, who placed himself in the middle, holding the necromancer by the coat, and me by the cloak...Two of the demons whom we had seen at the amphitheatre, went on before us leaping and skipping, sometimes running upon the roofs of the houses, and sometimes on the ground. The priest declared that, as often as he had entered magic circles, nothing so extraordinary had ever happened to him. As we went along, he would fain have persuaded me to assist at the consecrating a book, from which he said we should derive immense riches. We should then ask the demons to discover to us the various treasures with which the earth abounds, which would raise us to opulence and power; but that those love-affairs were mere follies from which no good could be expected. I made answer, that I would readily have accepted his

177

proposal if I had understood Latin…Immediately subsequent to this scene, Cellini got into one of those
scrapes, in which he was so frequently involved by his
own violence and ferocity; and the connection was
never again renewed.

The first remark that arises out of this narrative is,
that nothing is actually done by the supernatural personages which are exhibited. The magician reports
certain answers as given by the demons; but these
answers do not appear to have been heard from any
lips but those of him who was the creator or cause of
the scene. The whole of the demons therefore were
merely figures, produced by the magic lantern (which
is said to have been invented by Roger Bacon), or
by something of that nature. The burning of the perfumes served to produce a dense atmosphere, that was
calculated to exaggerate, and render more formidable
and terrific, the figures which were exhibited. The
magic lantern, which is now the amusement only of
servant-maids, and boys at school in their holidays,
served at this remote period, and when the power
of optical delusions was unknown, to terrify men of
wisdom and penetration, and make them believe that
legions of devils from the infernal regions were come
among them, to produce the most horrible effects, and
suspend and invert the laws of nature. It is probable,
that the magician, who carried home with him a "wallet full of books," also carried at the same time the
magic lantern or mirror, with its lights, which had
served him for his exhibition, and that this was the

cause of the phenomenon, that they observed two of the demons which they had seen at the amphitheatre, going before them on their return, "leaping and skipping, sometimes running on the roofs of the houses, and sometimes on the ground..."

Doctor Dee.

Dr. John Dee was a man who made a conspicuous figure in the sixteenth century. He was born at London in the year 1527. He was an eminent mathematician, and an indefatigable scholar. He says of himself, that, having been sent to Cambridge when he was fifteen, he persisted for several years in allowing himself only four hours for sleep in the twenty-four, and two for food and refreshment, and that he constantly occupied the remaining eighteen (the time for divine service only excepted) in study. At Cambridge he superintended the exhibition of a Greek play of Aristophanes, among the machinery of which he introduced an artificial scarabaeus, or beetle, which flew up to the palace of Jupiter, with a man on his back, and a basket of provisions. The ignorant and astonished spectators ascribed this feat to the arts of the magician...

The principal study of Dee however at this time lay in astrology; and accordingly, upon the accession of Elizabeth, Robert Dudley, her chief favourite, was sent to consult the doctor as to the aspect of the stars, that they might fix on an auspicious day for celebrating her coronation. Some years after we find him again on the continent; and in 1571, being taken ill at Louvaine, we are told the queen sent over two physicians to accomplish his cure. Elizabeth afterwards visited him at his house at Mortlake, that she might view his magazine of mathematical instruments and curiosities; and about this time employed him to defend her title to countries discovered in different parts of the globe. He says of himself, that he received the most advantageous offers from Charles V, Ferdinand, Maximilian II, and Rodolph II, emperors of Germany, and from the czar of Muscovy an offer of L.2000 sterling per annum, upon condition that he would reside in his dominions...

Had Dee gone no further than this, he would undoubtedly have ranked among the profoundest scholars and most eminent geniuses that adorned the reign of the maiden queen. But he was unfortunately cursed with an ambition that nothing could satisfy; and, having accustomed his mind to the wildest reveries, and wrought himself up to an extravagant pitch of enthusiasm, he pursued a course that involved him in much calamity, and clouded all his latter days with misery and ruin. He dreamed perpetually of the philosopher's stone, and was haunted with the belief of intercourse of a supramundane character. It is almost impossible to decide among these things, how much was illusion, and how much was forgery. Both were inextricably mixed in his proceedings; and this extraordinary victim probably could not in his most dispassionate moments precisely distinguish what belonged to the one, and what to the other.

As Dee was an enthusiast, so he perpetually interposed in his meditations prayers of the greatest emphasis and fervour. As he was one day in November 1582, engaged in these devout exercises, he says that there appeared to him the angel Uriel at the west window of his Museum, who gave him a translucent stone, or chrystal, of a convex form, that had the quality, when intently surveyed, of presenting apparitions, and even emitting sounds, in consequence of which the observer could hold conversations, ask questions and receive answers from the figures he saw in the mirror. It was often necessary that the stone should be turned one way and another in different positions, before the person who consulted it gained the right focus; and then the objects to be observed would sometimes shew themselves on the surface of the stone, and sometime in different parts of the room by virtue of the action of the stone. It had also this peculiarity, that only one person, having been named as seer, could see the figures exhibited, and hear the voices that spoke, though there might be various persons in the room. It appears that the person who discerned these visions must have his eyes and his ears uninterruptedly engaged in the affair, so that, as Dee experienced, to render the communication effectual, there must be two human beings concerned in the scene, one of them to describe what he saw, and to recite the dialogue that took place, and the other immediately to commit to paper all that his partner dictated. Dee for some reason chose for himself the part of the amanuensis, and had to seek for a companion, who was to watch the stone, and repeat to him whatever he saw and heard.

It happened opportunely that, a short time before Dee received this gift from on high, he contracted a familiar intercourse with one Edward Kelly of Worcestershire, whom he found specially qualified to perform the part which it was necessary to Dee to have adequately filled. Kelly was an extraordinary character, and in some respects exactly such a person as Dee wanted. He was just twenty-eight years younger than the memorable personage, who now received him as an inmate, and was engaged in his service at a stipulated salary of fifty pounds a year...

The first record of their consultations with the supramundane spirits, was of the date of December 2, 1581, at Lexden Heath in the county of Essex; and from this time they went on in a regular series of consultations with and enquiries from these miraculous visitors, a great part of which will appear to the uninitiated extremely puerile and ludicrous, but which were committed to writing with the most scrupulous exactness by Dee...

Kelly and Dee had not long been engaged in these supernatural colloquies, before an event occurred which gave an entirely new turn to their proceedings. Albert Alaski, a Polish nobleman, lord palatine of the principality of Siradia, came over at this time into

England, urged, as he said, by a desire personally to acquaint himself with the glories of the reign of Elizabeth, and the evidences of her unrivalled talents....

Alaski was extremely desirous to look into the womb of time; and Dee, it is likely, suggested repeated hints of his extraordinary power from his possession of the philosopher's stone. After two or three interviews, and much seeming importunity on the part of the Pole, Dee and Kelly graciously condescended to admit Alaski as a third party to their secret meetings with their supernatural visitors, from which the rest of the world were carefully excluded. Here the two Englishmen made use of the vulgar artifice, of promising extraordinary good fortune to the person of whom they purposed to make use. By the intervention of the miraculous stone they told the wondering traveller, that he should shortly become king of Poland, with the accession of several other kingdoms, that he should overcome many armies of Saracens and Paynims, and prove a mighty conqueror. Dee at the same time complained of the disagreeable condition in which he was at home, and that Burleigh and Walsingham were his malicious enemies. At length they concerted among themselves, that they, Alaski, and Dee and Kelly with their wives and families, should clandestinely withdraw out of England, and proceed with all practicable rapidity to Alaski's territory in the kingdom of Poland. They embarked on this voyage 21 September, and arrived at Siradia the third of February following.

At this place however the strangers remained little more than a month. Alaski found his finances in such disorder, that it was scarcely possible for him to feed the numerous guests he had brought along with him. The promises of splendid conquests which Dee and Kelly profusely heaped upon him, were of no avail to supply the deficiency of his present income. And the elixir they brought from Glastonbury was, as they said, so incredibly rich in virtue, that they were compelled to lose much time in making projection by way of trial, before they could hope to arrive at the proper temperament for producing the effect they desired.

In the following month Alaski with his visitors passed to Cracow, the residence of the kings of Poland. Here they remained five months, Dee and Kelly perpetually amusing the Pole with the extraordinary virtue of the stone, which had been brought from heaven by an angel, and busied in a thousand experiments with the elixir, and many tedious preparations which they pronounced to be necessary, before the compound could have the proper effect. The prophecies were uttered with extreme confidence; but no external indications were afforded, to shew that in any way they were likely to be realised. The experiments and exertions of the laboratory were incessant; but no transmutation was produced...Finally the zeal of Alaski diminished; he had no longer the same faith in the projectors that had deluded him; and he devised a way of sending them forward with letters of recommendation to Rodolph

184

II, emperor of Germany, at his imperial seat of
Prague...

...The final result was that Rodolph declined any
further intercourse with Dee. He turned a deaf ear to
his prophecies, and professed to be altogether void of
faith as to his promises respecting the philosopher's
stone. Dee however was led on perpetually with hopes
of better things from the emperor, till the spring of
the year 1585. At length he was obliged to fly from
Prague, the bishop of Placentia, the pope's nuncio,
having it in command from his holiness to represent
to Rodolph how discreditable it was for him to har-
bour English magicians, heretics, at his court.

From Prague Dee and his followers proceeded to
Cracow. Here he found means of introduction to
Stephen, king of Poland, to whom immediately he
insinuated as intelligence from heaven, that Rodolph,
the emperor, would speedily be assassinated, and that
Stephen would succeed him in the throne of Germany. Stephen appears to have received Dee with
more condescension than Rodolph had done, and was
once present at his incantation and interview with the
invisible spirits. Dee also lured him on with promises
respecting the philosopher's stone. Meanwhile the
magician was himself reduced to the strangest expedi-
ents for subsistence. He appears to have daily expected
great riches from the transmutation of metals, and was
unwilling to confess that he and his family were in the
mean time almost starving.

When king Stephen at length became wearied with

fruitless expectation, Dee was fortunate enough to meet with another and more patient dupe in Rosenburg, a nobleman of considerable wealth at Trebona in the kingdom of Bohemia. Here Dee appears to have remained till 1589, when he was sent for home by Elizabeth. In what manner he proceeded during this interval, and from whence he drew his supplies, we are only left to conjecture. He lured on his victim with the usual temptation, promising him that he should be king of Poland. In the mean time it is recorded by him, that, on the ninth of December, 1586, he arrived at the point of projection, having cut a piece of metal out of a brass warming-pan; and merely heating it by the fire, and pouring on it a portion of the elixir, it was presently converted into pure silver. We are told that he sent the warming-pan and the piece of silver to queen Elizabeth, that she might be convinced by her own eyes how exactly they tallied, and that the one had unquestionably been a portion of the other. About the same time it is said, that Dee and his associate became more free in their expenditure; and in one instance it is stated as an example, that Kelly gave away to the value of four thousand pounds sterling in gold rings on occasion of the celebration of the marriage of one of his maid-servants. On the twenty-seventh and thirtieth of July, 1587, Dee has recorded in his journal his gratitude to God for his unspeakable mercies on those days imparted, which has been interpreted to mean further acquisitions of wealth by means of the elixir...

It is not easy to imagine a state of greater degradation than that into which this person had now fallen. During all the prime and vigour of his intellect, he had sustained an eminent part among the learned and the great, distinguished and honoured by Elizabeth and her favourite. But his unbounded arrogance and self-opinion could never be satisfied. And seduced, partly by his own weakness, and partly by the insinuations of a crafty adventurer, he became a mystic of the most dishonourable sort. He was induced to believe in a series of miraculous communications without common sense, engaged in the pursuit of the philosopher's stone, and no doubt imagined that he was possessed of the great secret. Stirred up by these conceptions, he left his native country, and became a wanderer, preying upon the credulity of one prince and eminent man after another, and no sooner was he discarded by one victim of credulity, than he sought another, a vagabond on the earth, reduced from time to time to the greatest distress, persecuted, dishonoured and despised by every party in their turn. At length by incessant degrees he became dead to all moral distinctions, and all sense of honour and self-respect...

Led on as Dee at this time was by the ascendancy and consummate art of Kelly, there was far from existing any genuine harmony between them; and, after many squabbles and heart-burnings, they appear finally to have parted in January 1589, Dee having, according to his own account, at that time delivered up to Kelly, the elixir and the different implements by which the transmutation of metals was to be effected.

Various overtures appear to have passed now for some years between Dee and queen Elizabeth, intended to lead to his restoration to his native country. Dee had upon different occasions expressed a wish to that effect; and Elizabeth in the spring of 1589 sent him a message, that removed from him all further thought of hesitation and delay...She gave special orders, that he should do what he would in chemistry and philosophy, and that no one should on any account molest him.

But here end the prosperity and greatness of this extraordinary man. If he possessed the power of turning all baser metals into gold, he certainly acted unadvisedly in surrendering this power to his confederate, immediately before his return to his native country. He parted at the same time with his gift of prophecy, since, though he brought away with him his miraculous stone, and at one time appointed one Bartholomew, and another one Hickman, his interpreters to look into the stone, to see the marvellous sights it was expected to disclose, and to hear the voices and report the words that issued from it, the experiments proved in both instances abortive. They wanted the finer sense, or the unparalleled effrontery and inexhaustible invention, which Kelly alone possessed.

The remainder of the voyage of the life of Dee was "bound in shallows and in miseries." Queen Elizabeth we may suppose soon found that her dreams of immense wealth to be obtained through his intervention were nugatory. Yet would she not desert the favourite of her former years. He presently began to complain of poverty and difficulties. He represented that the revenue of two livings he held in the church had been withheld from him from the time of his going abroad. He stated that, shortly after that period, his house had been broken into and spoiled by a lawless mob, instigated by his ill fame as a dealer in prohibited and unlawful arts. They destroyed or dispersed his library, consisting of four thousand volumes, seven hundred of which were manuscripts, and of inestimable rarity. They ravaged his collection of curious implements and machines. He enumerated the expences of his journey home by Elizabeth's command, for which he seemed to consider the queen as his debtor. Elizabeth in consequence ordered him at several times two or three small sums. But this being insufficient, she was prevailed upon in 1592 to appoint two members of her privy council to repair to his house at Mortlake to enquire into particulars, to whom he made a Compendious Rehearsal of half a hundred years of his life, accompanied with documents and vouchers.

It is remarkable that in this Rehearsal no mention occurs of the miraculous stone brought down to him by an angel, or of his pretensions respecting the transmutation of metals. He merely rests, his claims to public support upon his literary labours, and the acknowledged eminence of his intellectual faculties. He passes over the years he had lately spent in foreign countries, in entire silence, unless we except his account of the particulars of his journey home…At length he receded altogether from public life, and retired to his ancient domicile at Mortlake. He made one attempt to propitiate the favour of king James; but it was ineffectual…

The history of Dee is exceedingly interesting, not only on its own account; not only for the eminence of his talents and attainments, and the incredible sottishness and blindness of understanding which marked his maturer years; but as strikingly illustrative of the credulity and superstitious faith of the time in which he lived. At a later period his miraculous stone which displayed such wonders, and was attended with so long a series of supernatural vocal communications would have deceived nobody: it was scarcely more ingenious than the idle tricks of the most ordinary conjurer. But at this period the crust of long ages of darkness had not yet been fully worn away. Men did not trust to the powers of human understanding, and were not familiarised with the main canons of evidence and belief. Dee passed six years on the continent, proceeding from the court of one prince or potent nobleman to another, listened to for a time by each, each regarding his oracular communications with astonishment and alarm, and at length irresolutely casting him off, when he found little or no difficulty in running a like career with another…

12

King James & Matthew Hopkins: Witch Finders

By now readers are no doubt tired of Godwin's refrain that *supposed access to occult power corrupted most necromancers beyond redemption.* During the Renaissance, intellectuals discovered and widely publicized the natural, mechanical, and technological sources of previously mysterious phenomenon by interrogating the historical record and subjecting it to the light of reason. The Scientific Revolution and Enlightenment continued this process, severing the once-strong link between the practice of witchcraft and the actual wielding of political power. As the politically and economically powerful ceased to be terrified, impressed, or inspired by occultic ravings, the magicians receded in social, academic, and political status to the position of an extremely lonesome minority of religious believers and peripatetic con men. As magic lost its power in European courts, it retained command of the average person's worldview. For the uneducated, the world still abounded with spirits, strange energies, and endless signs of Satan's battle against God. In the transitional Early Modern Period, monarchs like James I of Scotland and England could exploit the marginality of witches for his own political purposes. A particularly literary monarch, James wrote his own *Demonology* and orchestrated show trials for accused witches whom he perceived to have wronged him in some way or another. Individuals like Agnes Sampson and John Fian stood accused of causing a storm to delay the king's travel to Norway (where he was betrothed to marry). For their crimes, they suffered horrifying torture and execution.

Though James seems to have had a sort of empiricist change of heart by the end of his life, the backward example of his administration and 'scholarship' were invaluable to future bad actors like the "Witch Hunter" Matthew Hopkins. Throughout his bloody career (which flourished in the early days of England's Civil War), Hopkins traveled through England convincing localities that witch training grounds existed in their midst and Satan was actively attempting to invade the village. Hopkins' solution was for the towns to hire his Hunters to murder over 300 women accused of making satanic pacts. His reign of terror over just two years exterminated more marginalized people than the previous two centuries of witch-hunting in England. Having built a dandy career out of the horrible affair, Hopkins published his manual *The Discovery of Witches* in 1647. Within a few decades, the practice spread across the Atlantic to yet *another* Puritan society which seemed to have gone *insane.* For our final entries, we will turn to the infamous New England witch trials and our author's conclusions.

Sanguinary Proceedings against Witchcraft.

King James's Voyage to Norway.

While Elizabeth amused herself with the supernatural gifts to which Dee advanced his claim, and consoled the adversity and destitution to which the old man, once so extensively honoured, was now reduced, a scene of a very different complexion was played in the northern part of the island. Trials for sorcery were numerous in the reign of Mary queen of Scots; the comparative darkness and ignorance of the sister kingdom rendered it a soil still more favourable than England to the growth of these gloomy superstitions. But the mind of James, at once inquisitive, pedantic and self-sufficient, peculiarly fitted him for the pursuit of these narrow-minded and obscure speculations.

193

One combination of circumstances wrought up this propensity within him to the greatest height.

James was born in the year 1566. He was the only direct heir to the crown of Scotland; and he was in near prospect of succession to that of England. The zeal of the Protestant Reformation had wrought up the anxiety of men's minds to a fever of anticipation and forecast. Consequently, towards the end of the reign of Elizabeth, a point which greatly arrested the general attention was the expected marriage of the king of Scotland. Elizabeth, with that petty jealousy which obscured the otherwise noble qualities of her spirit, sought to countermine this marriage, that her rival and expected successor might not be additionally graced with the honours of offspring…[James' visit to Norway to marry is interrupted by unusually violent weather and the trip must be abandoned. James returns in a rage.]

It happened that, soon after James's return to Scotland, one Geillis Duncan, a servant-maid, for the extraordinary circumstances that attended certain cures which she performed, became suspected of witchcraft. Her master questioned her on the subject; but she would own nothing. Perceiving her obstinacy, the master took upon himself of his own authority, to extort confession from her by torture. In this he succeeded; and, having related divers particulars of witchcraft of herself, she proceeded to accuse others. The persons she accused were cast into the public prison.

One of these, Agnes Sampson by name, at first stoutly resisted the torture. But, it being more strenuously applied, she by and by became extremely communicative. It was at this period that James personally engaged in the examinations. We are told that he "took great delight in being present," and putting the proper questions. The unhappy victim was introduced into a room plentifully furnished with implements of torture, while the king waited in an apartment at a convenient distance, till the patient was found to be in a suitable frame of mind to make the desired communications. No sooner did he or she signify that they were ready, and should no longer refuse to answer, than they were introduced, fainting, sinking under recent sufferings which they had no longer strength to resist, into the royal presence. And here sat James, in envied ease and conscious "delight," wrapped up in the thought of his own sagacity, framing the enquiries that might best extort the desired evidence, and calculating with a judgment by no means to be despised, from the bearing, the turn of features, and the complexion of the victim, the probability whether he was making a frank and artless confession, or had still the secret desire to impose on the royal examiner, or from a different motive was disposed to make use of the treacherous authority which the situation afforded, to gratify his revenge upon some person towards whom he might be inspired with latent hatred and malice.

Agnes Sampson related with what solicitude she had sought to possess some fragment of the linen belonging to the king. If he had worn it, and it had contracted any soil from his royal person, this would be enough: she would infallibly, by applying her incantations to this fragment, have been able to undermine the life of the sovereign. She told how she with two hundred other witches had sailed in sieves from Leith to North Berwick church, how they had there encountered the devil in person, how they had feasted with him, and what obscenities had been practised. She related that in this voyage they had drowned a cat, having first baptised him, and that immediately a dreadful storm had arisen, and in this very storm the king's ship had been separated from the rest of his fleet. She took James aside, and, the better to convince him, undertook to repeat to him the conversation, the dialogue which had passed from the one to the other, between the king and queen in their bedchamber on the wedding-night. Agnes Sampson was condemned to the flames.

John Fian.

Another of the miserable victims on this occasion was John Fian, a schoolmaster at Tranent near Edinburgh, a young man, whom the ignorant populace had decorated with the style of doctor. He was tortured by means of a rope strongly twisted about his head, and by the boots. He was at length brought to confession. He told of a young girl, the sister of one of his scholars, with whom he had been deeply enamoured. He had proposed to the boy to bring him three hairs from the most secret part of his sister's body, possessing which he should be enabled by certain incantations to procure himself the love of the girl. The boy at his mother's instigation brought to Fian three hairs from a virgin heifer instead; and, applying his conjuration to them, the consequence had been that the heifer forced her way into his school, leaped upon him in amorous fashion, and would not be restrained from following him about the neighbourhood.

This same Fian acted an important part in the scene at North Berwick church. As being best fitted for the office, he was appointed recorder or clerk to the devil, to write down the names, and administer the oaths to the witches. He was actively concerned in the enchantment, by means of which the king's ship had nearly been lost on his return from Denmark. This part of his proceeding however does not appear in his own confession, but in that of the witches who were his fellow-conspirators.

He further said, that, the night after he made his confession, the devil appeared to him, and was in a furious rage against him for his disloyalty to his service, telling him that he should severely repent his infidelity. According to his own account, he stood firm, and defied the devil to do his worst. Meanwhile the next night he escaped out of prison, and was with some difficulty retaken. He however finally denied all his former confessions, said that they were falshoods forced from him by mere dint of torture, and, though

197

he was now once more subjected to the same treatment to such an excess as must necessarily have crippled him of his limbs for ever, he proved inflexible to the last. At length by the king's order he was strangled, and his body cast into the flames. Multitudes of unhappy men and women perished in this cruel persecution.

King James's Demonology.

It was by a train of observations and experience like this, that James was prompted seven years after to compose and publish his *Dialogues on Demonology in Three Books*. In the Preface to this book he says, "The fearfull abounding at this time in this countrey, of these detestable slaves of the Diuel, the Witches or enchaunters, hath moved me (beloued Reader) to dispatch in post this following Treatise of mine, not in any wise (as I protest) to serue for a shew of my learning and ingine, but onely (moued of conscience) to preasse thereby, so farre as I can, to resolue the doubting hearts of many, both that such assaults of Satan are most certainely practised, and that the instruments thereof merits most seuerely to be punished."

In the course of the treatise he affirms, "that barnes, or wiues, or neuer so diffamed persons, may serue for sufficient witnesses and proofes in such trialls; for who but Witches can be prooues, and so witnesses of the doings of Witches?" But, lest innocent persons should be accused, and suffer falsely, he tells us, "There are

198

two other good helps that may be used for their trial: the one is, the finding of their marke [a mark that the devil was supposed to impress upon some part of their persons], and the trying the insensibleness thereof: the other is their fleeting on the water: for, as in a secret murther, if the dead carkasse be at any time thereafter handled by the murtherer, it will gush out of bloud, as if the bloud were crying to the heauen for revenge of the murtherer, God hauing appointed that secret supernaturall signe, for triall of that secret unnaturall crime, so it appears that God hath appointed (for a supernaturall signe of the monstrous impietie of Witches) that the water shall refuse to receive them in her bosome, that haue shaken off them the sacred water of Baptisme, and wilfully refused the benefite thereof: No, not so much as their eyes are able to shed teares (threaten and torture them as ye please) while first they repent (God not permitting them to dissemble their obstinacie in so horrible a crime.)"

Statute, 1 James I.

In consequence of the strong conviction James entertained on the subject, the English parliament was induced, in the first year of his reign, to supersede the milder proceedings of Elizabeth, and to enact that "if any person shall use, practice, or exercise any invocation or conjuration of any evil and wicked spirit, or shall consult, covenant with, entertain, employ, feed or reward any evil and wicked spirit, to or for any intent and purpose; or take up any dead man, woman, or child out of their grave, or the skin, bone, or any part of any dead person, to be used in any manner of witchcraft, sorcery or enchantment, or shall use any witchcraft, sorcery or enchantment, whereby any person shall be killed, destroyed, wasted, consumed, pined or lamed in his or her body, or any part thereof; that then every such offender, their aiders, abettors and counsellors shall suffer the pains of death." And upon this statute great numbers were condemned and executed.

Latest Ideas of James on the Subject.

It is worthy of remark however that king James lived to alter his mind extremely on the question of witchcraft. He was active in his observations on the subject; and we are told that "the frequency of forged possessions which were detected by him wrought such an alteration in his judgment, that he, receding from what he had written in his early life, grew first diffident of, and then flatly to deny, the working of witches and devils, as but falshoods and delusions…"

Astrology.

The supposed science of astrology is of a nature less tremendous, and less appalling to the imagination, than the commerce with devils and evil spirits, or the raising of the dead from the peace of the tomb to effect certain magical operations, or to instruct the living as to the events that are speedily to befal them. Yet it is well worthy of attention in a work of this sort, if for no other reason, because it has prevailed in almost all nations and ages of the world, and has been assiduously cultivated by men, frequently of great talent, and who were otherwise distinguished for the soundness of their reasoning powers, and for the steadiness and perseverance of their application to the pursuits in which they engaged.

The whole of the question was built upon the supposed necessary connection of certain aspects and conjunctions or oppositions of the stars and heavenly bodies, with the events of the world and the characters and actions of men. The human mind has ever confessed an anxiety to pry into the future, and to deal in omens and prophetic suggestions, and, certain coincidences having occurred however fortuitously, to deduce from them rules and maxims upon which to build an anticipation of things to come.

Add to which, it is flattering to the pride of man, to suppose all nature concerned with and interested in what is of importance to ourselves...

The general belief in astrology had a memorable effect on the history of the human mind. All men in the first instance have an intuitive feeling of freedom in the acts they perform, and of consequence of praise or blame due to them in just proportion to the integrity or baseness of the motives by which they are actuated. This is in reality the most precious endowment of man. Hence it comes that the good man feels a pride and self-complacency in acts of virtue, takes credit to himself for the independence of his mind, and is conscious of the worth and honour to which he feels that he has a rightful claim. But, if all our acts are predetermined by something out of ourselves, if, however virtuous and honourable are our dispositions, we are overruled by our stars, and compelled to the acts, which, left to ourselves, we should most resolutely disapprove, our condition becomes slavery, and we are left in a state the most abject and hopeless. And, though our situation in this respect is merely imaginary, it does not the less fail to have very pernicious results to our characters. Men, so far as they are believers in astrology, look to the stars, and not to themselves, for an account of what they shall do, and resign themselves to the omnipotence of a fate which they feel it in vain to resist. Of consequence, a belief in astrology has the most unfavourable tendency as to the morality of man; and, were it not that the sense of the liberty of our actions is so strong that all the reasonings in the world cannot subvert it, there would be a fatal close to all human dignity and all human virtue...

Matthew Hopkins.

Nothing can place the credulity of the English nation on the subject of witchcraft about this time, in a more striking point of view, than the history of Matthew Hopkins, who, in a pamphlet published in 1647 in his own vindication, assumes to himself the surname of the Witch-finder. He fell by accident, in his native county of Suffolk, into contact with one or two reputed witches, and, being a man of an observing turn and an ingenious invention, struck out for himself a trade, which brought him such moderate returns as sufficed to maintain him, and at the same time gratified his ambition by making him a terror to many, and the object of admiration and gratitude to more, who felt themselves indebted to him for ridding them of secret and intestine enemies, against whom, as long as they proceeded in ways that left no footsteps behind, they felt they had no possibility of guarding themselves...

After two or three successful experiments, Hopkins engaged in a regular tour of the counties of Norfolk, Suffolk, Essex and Huntingdonshire. He united to him two confederates, a man named John Stern, and a woman whose name has not been handed down to us. They visited every town in their route that invited them, and secured to them the moderate remuneration of twenty shillings and their expences, leaving what was more than this to the spontaneous gratitude of those who should deem themselves indebted to the exertions of Hopkins and his party. By this expedient they secured to themselves a favourable reception; and a set of credulous persons who would listen to their dictates as so many oracles. Being three of them, they were enabled to play the game into one another's hands, and were sufficiently strong to overawe all timid and irresolute opposition. In every town to which they came, they enquired for reputed witches, and having taken them into custody, were secure for the most part of a certain number of zealous abettors, who took care that they should have a clear stage for their experiments. They overawed their helpless victims with a certain air of authority, as if they had received a commission from heaven for the discovery of misdeeds. They assailed the poor creatures with a multitude of questions constructed in the most artful manner. They stripped them naked, in search for the devil's marks in different parts of their bodies, which were ascertained by running pins to the head into those parts, that, if they were genuine marks, would prove themselves such by their insensibility. They swam their victims in rivers and ponds, it being an undoubted fact, that, if the persons accused were true witches, the water, which was the symbol of admission into the Christian church, would not receive them into its bosom. If the persons examined continued obstinate, they seated them in constrained and uneasy attitudes, occasionally binding them with cords, and compelling them to remain so without food or sleep for twenty-four hours. They walked them up and down the room, two taking them under each arm, till they dropped down with fatigue. They carefully swept the room in which the experiment was made, that they might keep away spiders and flies, which were supposed to be devils or their imps in that disguise.

The most plentiful inquisition of Hopkins and his confederates was in the years 1644, 1645 and 1646. At length there were so many persons committed to prison upon suspicion of witchcraft, that the government was compelled to take in hand the affair. The rural magistrates before whom Hopkins and his confederates brought their victims, were obliged, willingly or unwillingly, to commit them for trial...It may readily be believed, considering the temper of the times, that he insisted much upon the horrible nature of the sin of witchcraft, which could expect no pardon, either in this world or the world to come. He sat on the bench with the judges, and participated in their deliberations. In the result of this inquisition sixteen persons were hanged at Yarmouth in Norfolk, fifteen at Chelmsford, and sixty at various places in the county of Suffolk.

Whitlocke in his Memorials of English Affairs, under the date of 1649, speaks of many witches being apprehended about Newcastle, upon the information of a person whom he calls the Witch-finder, who, as his experiments were nearly the same, though he is not named, we may reasonably suppose to be Hopkins; and in the following year about Boston in Lincolnshire. In 1652 and 1653 the same author speaks of women in Scotland, who were put to incredible torture to extort from them a confession of what their adversaries imputed to them.

The fate of Hopkins was such us might be expected in similar cases. The multitude are at first impressed with horror at the monstrous charges that are advanced. They are seized, as by contagion, with terror at the mischiefs which seem to impend over them, and from which no innocence and no precaution appear to afford them sufficient protection. They hasten, as with an unanimous effort, to avenge themselves upon these malignant enemies, whom God and man alike combine to expel from society. But, after a time, they begin to reflect, and to apprehend that they have acted with too much precipitation, that they have been led on with uncertain appearances. They see one victim led to the gallows after another, without stint or limitation. They see one dying with the most solemn asseverations of innocence, and another confessing apparently she knows not what, what is put into her mouth by her relentless persecutors. They see these victims, old, crazy and impotent, harassed beyond endurance by the ingenious cruelties that are practised against them. They were first urged on by implacable hostility and fury, to be satisfied with nothing but blood. But humanity and remorse also have their turn. Dissatisfied with themselves, they are glad to point their resentment against another. The man that at first they hailed as a public benefactor, they presently come to regard with jealous eyes, and begin to consider as a cunning impostor, dealing in cool blood with the lives of his fellow-creatures for a paltry gain, and, still more horrible, for the lure of a perishable and short-lived fame. The multitude, we are told, after a few seasons, rose upon Hopkins, and resolved to subject him to one of his own criterions. They dragged him to a pond, and threw him into the water for a witch. It seems he floated on the surface, as a witch ought to do. They then pursued him with hootings and revilings, and drove him for ever into that obscurity and ignominy which he had amply merited...

13

Witch Trials in Sweden & Salem

Congratulations, patient reader! You have made it through to the end of Godwin's now revived *Lives of the Necromancers*. For our finale, we travel from Sweden in 1670 to Puritan New England a generation later. In our detour to Sweden, Godwin details the history of County Dalecarlia which today borders Norway in the central part of the country. Godwin assures us that the locals were your perfectly average sort of common folk, minding their own affairs, living and letting live. When a small coven of "witches" began expanding their numbers in the town of Mohra in 1670, however, it sent the locals into a frenzy.

The obviously troubled "witches" supposedly engaged in a variety of satanic festivities, dining with the devil himself on occasion. The devil commanded his witch envoys at Mohra to confiscate children from the village to expand the ranks of his followers. Hundreds of children fell ill with similar symptoms and "The whole town of Mohra became subject to the infection." The town petitioned the king for powers of inquiry into the matter and Charles XI established the necessary court. Godwin reports that the number of witches in Mohra rose from the original "two or three witches existing in some of the obscure quarters of this place" to *seventy* now tried by the court. Every single witch—including those who confessed and begged mercy—was executed. The court then turned on the children who confessed involvement in the witches' plot: Swedish authorities executed fifteen children and condemned fifty-six others to torture as retribution.

From Sweden, we shift to the infamous witch trials in Salem, Massachusetts in 1692. Godwin's theory of the Salem trials is representative of scholarly thought for quite some time: they were largely the result of a combination of personal animus, avarice, and cruelty within a deeply occultist culture. The Puritans were terribly fussy and moralizing people, by and large, and their history of Indian extermination and the destruction of alternative cultures in New England reflect their mystical worldview. True-believer Puritans saw Satan and his minions behind every tree and in the eyes of every person not Elect. They preached a creed of humility and righteousness so self-

assured that it easily translated into frenzied witch hunt-
ing. In fact, as we noted in our last chapter, many copies
of Matthew Hopkins' *The Discovery of Witches* rested (no
doubt with well-worn pages) on saints' bookshelves. Once
the first baseless accusations flew, the flood was unstop-
pable. As Godwin writes, "The accusations were of the
most vulgar and contemptible sort, invisible pinchings and
blows, fits, with the blastings and mortality of cattle, and
wains stuck fast in the ground, or losing their wheels." The
supposed victims claimed that *spectral forces which only the
accuser could see* terrorized them and vandalized their
property. On the basis of such outlandish testimony, New
England courts executed nineteen accused witches and
subjected many repenting convicts to purifying torture.
One thing finally ended the feverish trials: accusers gradually turned on the affluent and influential after using up
the easier targets of marginalized and poor women. Once
the Massachusetts Bay elite felt their interests also seriously threatened by the hysteric outbreak, they
reasserted control over the courts and ended the trials.

Finally, our author concludes that enough is enough with
the witches already! We are so fortunate as to live in an
age in which necromancers possess no supernatural powers nor do they have the ability to exploit significant portions of the population. Rather, knowledge and science
have advanced so far that we see through any potential
threat these individuals pose and indeed have even come
to pity the occultist and his decidedly *strange* persona.
Therefore, Godwin finishes, let us bask in the learning of

our age, never forgetting the ignorant depths to which humans can plunge, forever "harassed with imaginary terrors, and haunted by suggestions." Despite Godwin's optimism, though, modern readers may leave this volume uncomfortably aware that we, too, have our true believers, necromancers, and persecutionists—they are the technocrats, the statist-futurists, the millennial and post-millennial pietists, the delusional post-Soviet socialists, the corporatists, professional academia (itself a monopolistic and calcifying living fossil from the medieval period); they are the constant doom-sayers, and the hordes of political hucksters worshipping at the altar of Keynesian calculationism, the protectionists, and the cultural mytho-nationalists (to name a few). Humanity's raw intelligence has indeed increased *dramatically* from the ancient era to the present—especially so in the years since Godwin's death—but true progress remains unevenly distributed.

Sanguinary Proceedings against Witchcraft.

Witchcraft in Sweden.

The story of witchcraft, as it is reported to have passed in Sweden in the year 1670, and has many times been reprinted in this country, is on several accounts one of the most interesting and deplorable that has ever been recorded. The scene lies in Dalecarlia, a country for ever memorable as having witnessed some of the earliest adventures of Gustavus Vasa, his deepest humiliation, and the first commencement of his prosperous fortune. The Dalecarlians are represented to us as the simplest, the most faithful, and the bravest of the sons of men, men undebauched and unsuspicious, but who devoted themselves in the most disinterested manner for a cause that appeared to them worthy of support, the cause of liberty and independence against the cruelest of tyrants…

The Dalecarlians, simple and ignorant, but of exemplary integrity and honesty, who dwelt amidst impracticable mountains and spacious mines of copper and iron, were distinguished for superstition among the countries of the north, where all were superstitious. They were probably subject at intervals to the periodical visitation of alarms of witches, when whole races of men became wild with the infection without any one's being well able to account for it.

In the year 1670, and one or two preceding years, there was a great alarm of witches in the town of Mohra. There were always two or three witches existing in some of the obscure quarters of this place. But now they increased in number, and shewed their faces with the utmost audacity. Their mode on the present occasion was to make a journey through the air to Blockula, an imaginary scene of retirement, which none but the witches and their dupes had ever seen. Here they met with feasts and various entertainments,

212

which it seems had particular charms for the persons who partook of them. The witches used to go into a field in the environs of Mohra, and cry aloud to the devil in a peculiar sort of recitation, "Antecessor, come and carry us to Blockula!" Then appeared a multitude of strange beasts, men, spits, posts, and goats with spits run through their entrails and projecting behind that all might have room. The witches mounted these beasts of burthen or vehicles, and were conveyed through the air over high walls and mountains, and through churches and chimneys, without perceptible impediment, till they arrived at the place of their destination. Here the devil feasted them with various compounds and confections, and, having eaten to their hearts' content, they danced, and then fought. The devil made them ride on spits, from which they were thrown; and the devil beat them with the spits, and laughed at them. He then caused them to build a house to protect them against the day of judgment, and presently overturned the walls of the house, and derided them again. All sorts of obscenities were reported to follow upon these scenes. The devil begot on the witches sons and daughters: this new generation intermarried again, and the issue of this further conjunction appears to have been toads and serpents. How all this pedigree proceeded in the two or three years in which Blockula had ever been heard of, I know not that the witches were ever called on to explain.

But what was most of all to be deplored, the devil

was not content with seducing the witches to go and celebrate this infernal sabbath; he further insisted that they should bring the children of Mohra along with them. At first he was satisfied, if each witch brought one; but now he demanded that each witch should bring six or seven for her quota. How the witches managed with the minds of the children we are at a loss to guess. These poor, harmless innocents, steeped to the very lips in ignorance and superstition, were by some means kept in continual alarm by the wicked, or, to speak more truly, the insane old women, and said as their prompters said. It does not appear that the children ever left their beds, at the time they reported they had been to Blockula. Their parents watched them with fearful anxiety. At a certain time of the night the children were seized with a strange shuddering, their limbs were agitated, and their skins covered with a profuse perspiration. When they came to themselves, they related that they had been to Blockula, and the strange things they had seen, similar to what had already been described by the women. Three hundred children of various ages are said to have been seized with this epidemic.

The whole town of Mohra became subject to the infection, and were overcome with the deepest affliction. They consulted together, and drew up a petition to the royal council at Stockholm, intreating that they would discover some remedy, and that the government would interpose its authority to put an end to a calamity to which otherwise they could find no limit.

The king of Sweden was at that time Charles the Eleventh, father of Charles the Twelfth, and was only fourteen years of age. His council in their wisdom deputed two commissioners to Mohra, and furnished them with powers to examine witnesses, and to take whatever proceedings they might judge necessary to put an end to so unspeakable a calamity.

They entered on the business of their commission on the thirteenth of August, the ceremony having been begun with two sermons in the great church of Mohra, in which we may be sure the damnable sin of witchcraft was fully dilated on, and concluding with prayers to Almighty God that in his mercy he would speedily bring to an end the tremendous misfortune, with which for their sins he had seen fit to afflict the poor people of Mohra. The next day they opened their commission. Seventy witches were brought before them. They were all at first stedfast in their denial, alleging that the charges were wantonly brought against them, solely from malice and ill will. But the judges were earnest in pressing them, till at length first one, and then another; burst into tears, and confessed all. Twenty-three were prevailed on thus to disburthen their consciences; but nearly the whole, as well those who owned the justice of their sentence, as those who protested their innocence to the last, were executed. Fifteen children confessed their guilt, and were also executed. Thirty-six other children (who we may infer did not confess), between the ages of nine and sixteen, were condemned to run the gauntlet, and to be whipped on their hands at the church-door every Sunday for a year together. Twenty others were whipped on their hands for three Sundays.

This is certainly a very deplorable scene, and is made the more so by the previous character which history has impressed on us, of the simplicity, integrity, and generous love of liberty of the Dalecarlians. For the children and their parents we can feel nothing but unmingled pity. The case of the witches is different. That three hundred children should have been made the victims of this imaginary witchcraft is doubtless a grievous calamity. And that a number of women should have been found so depraved and so barbarous, as by their incessant suggestions to have practised on the minds of these children, so as to have robbed them of sober sense, to have frightened them into fits and disease, and made them believe the most odious impossibilities, argued a most degenerate character, and well merited severe reprobation, but not death. Add to which, many of these women may be believed innocent, otherwise a great majority of those who were executed, would not have died protesting their entire freedom from what was imputed to them. Some of the parents no doubt, from folly and ill judgment, aided the alienation of mind in their children which they afterwards so deeply deplored, and gratified their senseless aversion to the old women, when they were themselves in many cases more the real authors of the evil than those who suffered.

Witchcraft in New England.

As a story of witchcraft, without any poetry in it, without any thing to amuse the imagination, or interest the fancy, but hard, prosy, and accompanied with all that is wretched, pitiful and withering, perhaps the well known story of the New England witchcraft surpasses every thing else upon record. The New Englanders were at this time, towards the close of the seventeenth century, rigorous Calvinists, with long sermons and tedious monotonous prayers, with hell before them for ever on one side, and a tyrannical, sour and austere God on the other, jealous of an arbitrary sovereignty, who hath "mercy on whom he will have mercy, and whom he will he hardeneth." These men, with long and melancholy faces, with a drawling and sanctified tone, and a carriage that would "at once make the most severely disposed merry, and the most cheerful spectators sad," constituted nearly the entire population of the province of Massachusetts Bay.

The prosecutions for witchcraft continued with little intermission principally at Salem, during the greater part of the year 1692. The accusations were of the most vulgar and contemptible sort, invisible pinchings and blows, fits, with the blastings and mortality of cattle, and wains stuck fast in the ground, or losing their wheels. A conspicuous feature in nearly the whole of these stories was what they named the "spectral sight;" in other words, that the profligate accusers first feigned for the most part the injuries they received, and next saw the figures and action of the persons who inflicted them, when they were invisible to every one else. Hence the miserable prosecutors gained the power of gratifying the wantonness of their malice, by pretending that they suffered by the hand of any one whose name first presented itself, or against whom they bore an ill will. The persons so charged, though unseen by any but the accuser, and who in their corporal presence were at a distance of miles, and were doubtless wholly unconscious of the mischief that was hatching against them, were immediately taken up, and cast into prison. And what was more monstrous and incredible, there stood at the bar the prisoner on trial for his life, while the witnesses were permitted to swear that his spectre had haunted them, and afflicted them with all manner of injuries. That the poor prosecuted wretch stood astonished at what was alleged against him, was utterly overwhelmed with the charges, and knew not what to answer, was all of it interpreted as so many presumptions of his guilt. Ignorant as they were, they were unhappy and unskilful in their defence; and, if they spoke of the devil, as was but natural, it was instantly caught at as a proof how familiar they were with the fiend that had seduced them to their damnation.

The first specimen of this sort of accusation in the present instance was given by one Paris, minister of a church at Salem, in the end of the year 1691, who had two daughters, one nine years old, the other eleven, that were afflicted with fits and convulsions. The first person fixed on as the mysterious author of what was seen, was Tituba, a female slave in the family, and she was harassed by her master into a confession of unlawful practices and spells. The girls then fixed on Sarah Good, a female known to be the victim of a morbid melancholy, and Osborne, a poor man that had for a considerable time been bed-rid, as persons whose spectres had perpetually haunted and tormented them: and Good was twelve months after hanged on this accusation.

A person, who was one of the first to fall under the imputation, was one George Burroughs, also a minister of Salem. He had, it seems, buried two wives, both of whom the busy gossips said he had used ill in their life-time, and consequently, it was whispered, had murdered them. This man was accustomed foolishly to vaunt that he knew what people said of him in his absence; and this was brought as a proof that he dealt with the devil. Two women, who were witnesses against him, interrupted their testimony with exclaiming that they saw the ghosts of the murdered wives present (who had promised them they would come), though no one else in the court saw them; and this was taken in evidence. Burroughs conducted himself in a very injudicious way on his trial; but, when he came to be hanged, made so impressive a speech on the ladder, with fervent protestations of innocence, as melted many of the spectators into tears.

The nature of accusations of this sort is ever found to operate like an epidemic. Fits and convulsions are communicated from one subject to another. The "spectral sight," as it was called, is obviously a theme for the vanity of ignorance...When too such things are talked of, when the devil and spirits of hell are made familiar conversation, when stories of this sort are among the daily news, and one person and another, who had a little before nothing extraordinary about them, become subjects of wonder, these topics enter into the thoughts of many, sleeping and waking: "their young men see visions, and their old men dream dreams."

In such a town as Salem, the second in point of importance in the colony, such accusations spread with wonderful rapidity. Many were seized with fits, exhibited frightful contortions of their limbs and features, and became a fearful spectacle to the bystander. They were asked to assign the cause of all this; and they supposed, or pretended to suppose, some neighbour, already solitary and afflicted, and on that account in ill odour with the townspeople, scowling upon, threatening, and tormenting them. Presently persons, specially gifted with the "spectral sight," formed a class by themselves, and were sent about at the public expence from place to place, that they might see what no one else could see. The prisons were filled with the persons accused. The utmost horror was entertained, as of a calamity which in such a degree had never visited that part of the world. It happened, most unfortunately, that Baxter's *Certainty of the World of Spirits* had been published but the year before, and a number of copies had been sent out to New England. There seemed a strange coincidence and sympathy between vital Christianity in its most honourable sense, and the fear of the devil, who appeared to be "come down unto them, with great wrath." Mr. Increase Mather, and Mr. Cotton Mather, his son, two clergymen of highest reputation in the neighbourhood, by the solemnity and awe with which they treated the subject, and the earnestness and zeal which they displayed, gave a sanction to the lowest superstition and virulence of the ignorant.

All the forms of justice were brought forward on this occasion. There was no lack of judges, and grand juries, and petty juries, and executioners, and still less of prosecutors and witnesses. The first person that was hanged was on the tenth of June, five more on the nineteenth of July, five on the nineteenth of August, and eight on the twenty-second of September. Multitudes confessed that they were witches; for this appeared the only way for the accused to save their lives. Husbands and children fell down on their knees, and implored their wives and mothers to own their guilt. Many were tortured by being tied neck and heels together, till they confessed whatever was suggested to them. It is remarkable however that not one persisted in her confession at the place of execution...

The whole of this dreadful tragedy was kept together by a thread. The spectre-seers for a considerable time prudently restricted their accusations to persons of ill repute, or otherwise of no conse-

221

quence in the community. By and by however they lost sight of this caution, and pretended they saw the figures of some persons well connected, and of unquestioned honour and reputation, engaged in acts of witchcraft. Immediately the whole fell through in a moment. The leading inhabitants presently saw how unsafe it would be to trust their reputations and their lives to the mercy of these profligate accusers. Of fifty-six bills of indictment that were offered to the grand-jury on the third of January, 1693, twenty-six only were found true bills, and thirty thrown out. On the twenty-six bills that were found, three persons only were pronounced guilty by the petty jury, and these three received their pardon from the government. The prisons were thrown open; fifty confessed witches, together with two hundred persons imprisoned on suspicion, were set at liberty, and no more accusations were heard of. The "afflicted," as they were technically termed, recovered their health; the "spectral sight" was universally scouted; and men began to wonder how they could ever have been the victims of so horrible a delusion.

Conclusion.

The volume of records of supposed necromancy and witchcraft is sufficiently copious, without its being in any way necessary to trace it through its latest relics and fragments. Superstition is so congenial to the mind of man, that, even in the early years of the author of the present volume, scarcely a village was unfurnished with an old man or woman who laboured under an ill repute on this score; and I doubt not many remain to this very day. I remember, when a child, that I had an old woman pointed out to me by an ignorant servant-maid, as being unquestionably possessed of the ominous gift of the "evil eye," and that my impulse was to remove myself as quickly as might be from the range of her observation.

But witchcraft, as it appears to me, is by no means so desirable a subject as to make one unwilling to drop it. It has its uses. It is perhaps right that we should be somewhat acquainted with this repulsive chapter in the annals of human nature...But I feel no propensity to linger in these dreary abodes, and would rather make a speedy exchange for the dwellings of healthfulness and a certain hilarity. We will therefore with the reader's permission at length shut the book, and say, "Lo, it is enough."

There is no time perhaps at which we can more fairly quit the subject, than when the more enlightened governments of Europe have called for the code of their laws, and have obliterated the statute which annexed the penalty of death to this imaginary crime.

So early as the year 1672, Louis XIV promulgated an order of the council of state, forbidding the tribunals from proceeding to judgment in cases where the accusation was of sorcery only.

In England we paid a much later tribute to the progress of illumination and knowledge; and it was not till the year 1736 that a statute was passed, repealing the law made in the first year of James I, and enacting that no capital prosecution should for the future take place for conjuration, sorcery and enchantment, but restricting the punishment of persons pretending to tell fortunes and discover stolen goods by witchcraft, to that appertaining to a misdemeanour.

As long as death could by law be awarded against those who were charged with a commerce with evil spirits, and by their means inflicting mischief on their species, it is a subject not unworthy of grave argument and true philanthropy, to endeavour to detect the fallacy of such pretences, and expose the incalculable evils and the dreadful tragedies that have grown out of accusations and prosecutions for such imaginary crimes. But the effect of perpetuating the silly and superstitious tales that have survived this mortal blow, is exactly opposite. It only serves to keep alive the lingering folly of imbecile minds, and still to feed with pestiferous clouds the thoughts of the ignorant. Let us rather hail with heart-felt gladness the light which has, though late, broken in upon us, and weep over the calamity of our forefathers, who, in addition to the inevitable ills of our sublunary state, were harassed with imaginary terrors, and haunted by suggestions…

THE END.

Liberty. It's a simple idea and the linchpin of a complex system of values and practices: justice, prosperity, responsibility, toleration, cooperation, and peace. Many people believe that liberty is the core political value of modern civilization itself, the one that gives substance and form to all the other values of social life. They're called libertarians.

Libertarianism.org is the Cato Institute's treasury of resources about the theory and history of liberty. The book you're holding is a small part of what Libertarianism.org has to offer. In addition to hosting classic texts by historical libertarian figures and original articles from modern-day thinkers, Libertarianism.org publishes podcasts, videos, online introductory courses, and books on a variety of topics within the libertarian tradition.